Pilgrim Prayers
for Single Fathers

Pilgrim Prayers for Single Fathers

David Albert Farmer

WIPF & STOCK · Eugene, Oregon

Dedicated to:
Martha Farmer, *My Mother*
The late A. J. Farmer, *My Father*
Kim Dodson, *My Sister*
Greg Farmer, *My Brother*
Wonderful Parents All

Wipf and Stock Publishers
199 W 8th Ave, Suite 3
Eugene, OR 97401

Pilgrim Prayers for Single Fathers
By Farmer, David Albert
Copyright©2004 Pilgrim Press
ISBN 13: 978-1-60899-191-4
Publication date 11/17/2009
Previously published by Pilgrim Press, 2004

This limited edition licensed by special permission of The Pilgrim Press.

Contents

Preface / 7
Prayerful Proclivities: An Introduction / 11
1. Anticipation / 15
2. The Mystery of Life's Beginning / 18
3. Nonstop Reasons to Rejoice / 20
4. Damned Divorce / 23
5. "I Want Mommy" / 26
6. Going to Hell: Jesus Is Very Uncomfortable by Now / 28
7. Ebony and Ivory / 31
8. To Share or Not to Share / 34
9. Visits Back Home / 36
10. First Date . . . in a Looooooooong Time / 38
11. Bad Dreams / 40
12. Only Her Hairdresser Knows for Sure / 42
13. Morticia's Fierce Fans / 45
14. Tuna Pile / 47
15. I Need a Break / 50
16. My Child Is Caught in the Middle / 52
17. My New Love Interest / 55
18. A Very, Very Special Invitation to Come to School / 57
19. Money, Money, Mo . . . ney / 60
20. Who Opened the Window? / 64
21. They Skipped This in Parenting Classes! / 66

22. Martha Stewart Sure Don't Live Here! or
I Swear, the Underwear I Used as Pot Holders Were Clean! / 69

23. The "M" Word / 72

24. Ivory and Ebony / 76

25. Sup, Docs? / 79

26. The Best Sermon Ever / 82

27. A Death in the Family / 86

28. Reality Check / 90

29. The Buggy / 92

30. Moving Out / 95

31. Closing Prayer . . . for Now / 97

Appendix / 101

Preface

I ASSUME THAT IF YOU HAVE GOTTEN to this page in this book, you have some kind of an interest in the demanding, rewarding life of a single father. You may be the single father seeking some words of insight, encouragement, and support. Or you may be someone who knows a single father in need of something to help him face the tasks confronting him on a day-to-day basis with regard to the care of his child or children; maybe you are his parent, his sibling, his pastor, his friend, his professional colleague, or even his ex-mother-in-law.

For whatever reason, the book is now in your hands. Let me tell you right here that, yes, it's completely encouraging and affirming of single dads; there is no condemnation, not even a subtle slur about how he came to be a single father. How he got to be one of us is of no concern to me as long as he is able to treat himself and his child or children with respect and affection.

There are a variety of single fathers. Some are full-time single dads. Some take complete responsibility for the children every other night or so. Some are weekenders. As I write, the single fathers I have in mind are those who, beyond providing financial support, are actively involved in the rearing of their children as full-time or part-time solo parents.

More and more of us are popping up all the time, and most of us never gave a thought to embarking on child-rearing alone. We thought life with the kids would usually or always include life with mom, but did things ever change for us and for our kids! Now there are many aspects of raising children where mom isn't involved at all. Mom rears them when she has them, and dad rears them when he has them. When necessary, they may discuss matters requiring the approval of both parents, but otherwise when talking to mom, dad may be reminded that the divorce was for a reason (or several!).

On the other hand, dads may have their child or children to raise by themselves. The mother may be absent because of some tragedy caused by disease or accident. It may also be because of her choice not to be anything more than a biological mother; thus, dad becomes a full-time, overtime, 24/7 parent.

In all of these cases, dads, under heavy responsibilities, try to do their best. Applause is certainly in order.

This book is built on the assumption that a single father (and anyone else for that matter) can find his greatest source of strength for the undertaking of his responsibilities through communion with the God of love. Prayer (and I'm talking about authentic communion with God, not what most people seem to call "prayer" these days) is the key to such communion, and what you will find in the following pages are prayers written in a wide variety of circumstances—at moments of joy, at moments of frustration, at moments of confusion. You may make them your own words or use them to spring you into prayers of your own.

I have been a single father for some twelve years after having been married to the mother of my two sons for thirteen-and-a-half years. As I complete this manuscript, my boys are now young adults, one a recent college grad and one about halfway through college. They have tossed me a few curve balls along the way, and I them. Indeed, we have all had our differences, but the rough places were smoothed out as the years passed. Problems were solved and compromise put into place, not because any one of us always did the right thing or acted in selfless ways, but because amid all the sound and fury, we realized that we loved each other, and in the end nothing else mattered very much. There would be no need or inspiration for writing this book had it not been for my much loved and loving sons, Carson Gregory Farmer and Jarrett Logan Farmer.

I have relived many events as I wrote these prayers and gathered the support materials for each segment of the book. I have laughed and cried, felt disappointment and pride and exhilaration—emotions very much a part of single fatherhood in the real world. But at every pause on the pathway, I have given thanks to God for the indescribable privilege of fatherhood, including single fatherhood.

Additionally, as I wrote this book, I was able to rethink, in a focused way, about the people—family members, friends, and professionals—who cared about us in very real ways and who made a vital contribution to the boys' rearing and to my survival! I am also aware that the boys had a lot of "surviving" to do too. It is no easy task to grow up in the modern world with only one parent to help and support you. The challenge for children is intensified.

Let me offer a brief explanation concerning the format and content you are about to read. Nearly each incident to which I refer has some basis in reality—as hard as it may be to believe at points. I have changed many names to protect the innocent and the guilty, but no incident described or alluded to is purely fictional. The material in most sections is presented in a format used in The Pilgrim Press's previously published and very successful book of prayers for single mothers.

Specifically, each section of the book opens with a look into some real-life situations. I have elected to present many of these as letters I wrote (or thought about writing, or should have written). I am a big letter/e-mail writer, so this is natural and realistic for me. This is followed by a reference to a scripture passage from either the Hebrew Bible or Christian scriptures, a prayer related to the subject, and—finally—an excerpt from a written source that offers further clarity and/or a basis for further reflection/investigation.

I have relied on an array of sources, including some Internet resources, for these "further reflection/investigation" pieces. The reasons for this are twofold: 1) It's much easier for a writer to use multiple references on-line rather than search for the right book or journal in a library or bookstore; 2) Since some of the end-of-section references are related to advice and help, I have assumed that it would be easier for you, the reader, to find those materials on-line instead of having to search for them in a book. I'm expecting that this will happen with some frequency as you read.

Remember, if you're a single father, God did not will your divorce or the headache you may have received after listening to *Barney* with your kid. Neither are you a freak of nature or culture; you're one in a growing crowd.

I have to share something with you right now. The following information is in no way intended to put down single mothers. Many single mothers were and are true heroines, and historically have taken care of children who needed to be cared for after a divorce—often with little or no help from absentee and/or deadbeat dads. So hats off to single moms. Hey! They paved the way for excellence in single parenting.

Read the following promotional blurb about a 2001 book, *Father and Child Reunion,* by psychologist Warren Farrell, on single fatherhood:

> Based on thirteen years of research, *Father and Child Reunion* will force a re-examination of the circumstances in which a dad or a mom is best for children. For starters, some findings on children with single parents . . .

* Children do better with single fathers than with single mothers. Both boys and girls are healthier and do better psychologically and academically, as well as socially.
* Even characteristics such as empathy are exhibited more by children brought up by single fathers.
* Single fathers experience less stress juggling children and work than do single mothers.

What family structures are most likely to be in the child's best interests? Dr. Farrell's findings suggest the following ranking:

1. the intact family;
2. shared parent-time (joint physical custody);
3. primary father time;
4. primary mother time.

While the intact family is the winner, *Father and Child Reunion* makes it clear why, if divorce cannot be prevented, children being primarily with their dads gives children more of both parents than when they are primarily with their mothers; reduces a mother's economic dependency on a man, and reduces men's ten times greater suicide rate after divorce.

Source: http://www.shopnetdaily.com/store/item.asp?ITEM_ID=77&RELATED_ITEM_ID=46.

• • •

Again, cheers to single moms. I don't think we should create an "us against them" scenario, but I would like for Dr. Farrell's research and book to cause you to do some rethinking and to help convince you that you as a single father really do have the capacity of and the potential for rearing your child in a fully healthful and otherwise superb manner.

I hope you will be able to sense my concern for you and your kids as you read. Good parenting doesn't JUST happen; but it can happen, and it can happen in your home. I suspect, in the majority of cases, it already is. A new reliance on prayer for the journey will continue, and not begin, your quality approach to being a dad.

Most of all, I hope you will find new strength to help you do your best as a single dad in the care of your kids and yourself!

Prayerful Proclivities
An Introduction

As you read the prayers contained herein, you will notice rather quickly some of my biases about prayer, what it is and how to do it. Rather than assume that you'll finally catch on to my leanings in this regard, I want to take a small space to explain a few matters very directly.

My Biases about What Prayer Is (and What Prayer Is NOT)

We do not pray by accident or happenstance. Neither is simply speaking out loud (or silently) in what we may call "prayer," necessarily prayer at all.

Prayer may occur spontaneously, as when we can't help but offer praise to God, in hosts of possible ways, but it won't occur unless we want it to. Similarly, I'm amazed at the number of people who think God is just sitting around, waiting for them to utter something to which God is expected to respond. It's not that God has a special cell number that has to be dialed, and it's not that one has to say, "Okay, I'm going to be praying now." But real prayer does require a kind of tuning in; some might call this process "centering." What the process is called really doesn't matter at all, but I have noticed that those who are reported to have prayed in the pages of the Hebrew Bible and in Christian scripture usually came to their prayers with both a focus on God and an attentiveness to God's Spirit, which is the same thing as saying "God's presence." If there are any hey-you-prayers, I've missed them.

Not many of us, unless it's with spouses or partners and children whom we take for granted, just start talking without at least saying the name of the person to whom we want to speak. (Even if there are only two of you in the house these days, as you get older you still have to call the name of the person to whom you wish to speak so she or he will know that you want conversation and not another time to talk to yourself.) If we are not focused on God, if we are not concentrating on God, if we have not placed ourselves in a "space" for communion (and I'm not suggesting by any means that one has to go into a chapel or a closet to pray), then prayer will not take place. Talking to ourselves will occur, and that's all.

It's ridiculous to toss out something to God, as if God is your gopher or your genie, without being engaged consciously enough to receive some sense of leaning or leading in response. Equally ridiculous is the superstitious notion that even mindless prayer is a good thing or that prayer is a required thing to do, so we go through public and private rote prayers that stopped engaging our own consciousness years (and years!) ago.

Prayer is dynamic and real and enriching and surprising and, sometimes, shocking. God continuously pulls us all, individually and communally, toward everything that is whole and wholesome, and very often this means that God's pull of us is in a direction we hadn't even thought of going in search of our own wholeness. God is neither a yes-person nor a rubber stamp. God is no more a magician than God is a short-order cook.

Most significantly, God is not one of us. God is not a human being with our needs and our limitations and our often petty tendencies. God doesn't play favorites, and God doesn't have a preference for any particular continent on Planet Earth or, necessarily, for Planet Earth over any other places there might be life responding openly to the Creator.

My Biases about How to (and How NOT to) Pray

How NOT to Pray

1. Don't order God around; get rid of imperatives in prayer.
2. Don't approach God as if God needs or wants to be appeased.
3. Don't blame God for evil or tragedy.
4. Don't pray as if you have to talk God into doing what God hadn't already thought to do and isn't already in the process of trying to effect.
5. Don't bargain with God.
6. Don't tell God what needs to be done in a given situation.
7. Don't treat prayer as incantation.
8. Don't think of God as your grandfather or your grandmother (or any other person or kind of person, despite *Oh, God* and *Joan of Arcadia*).
9. Don't assume that anything or everything that happens is God's will, intentional or unintentional; there are realities of a physical uni-

verse (in which "errors" occur naturally) and of the power of individual and communal bad/selfish/evil choices.
10. Don't forget the fact that God is love—not just loving, but love.

How to Pray

1. Do base all prayer in praise of God.
2. Do pray thankfully for what God has already done and is doing.
3. Do pray as part of the one human family, recognizing that God neither recognizes nor approves of the barriers we human beings build between ourselves and other human beings.
4. Do pray directly to God, as Jesus did.
5. Do pray with utter openness in God's presence, leaving "pretense" and "oughtness" on the game shelf. Express to God, with words if you can, what you think your hurts and needs are (without feeling compelled to force or obligate God to act in the way you tell God things need to be done).
6. Do pray as an active participant in what happens to you, your loved ones, and your world.
7. Do pray with an awareness of God's extraordinary nearness.
8. Do learn from the prayers of others without being bound by them.
9. Do listen for and watch for evidences of God's responsiveness to your prayers in new understandings that seem to come to you out of nowhere, in strong feelings you hadn't felt or noticed that you'd felt before, and in bursts of energy to act or to endure that you're pretty sure you couldn't have mustered all by yourself.
10. Do set as your goal to pray without ceasing.

Each of these is explained in some detail in the Appendix. For now, I don't want to slow you down any more on your way to the prayers themselves.

Invocation

Gracious God,

I am profoundly grateful for your unwavering presence in my life and for the lessons I have learned about you and about prayer as you have walked with me and stood with me, cried with me and laughed with me all the days of my life. Among other things, O God, I consider myself most fortunate to have stumbled into the reality of prayer as constant communion, which helped me do away with the practice of prayer as an occasional or even a regularly scheduled brief chitchat.

I am grateful for the ways Jesus from Nazareth understood you and for all he did to cause others who would listen to look at you in a light that then was very new. I am, in addition, grateful for the exceptional opportunities I have had to read about and reflect on what other visionaries and seekers have discovered about you, and for sufficient-enough emotional health to be able to believe in and open myself to your love. The reality of how your presence and your power center me, strengthen me, and give me hope has not escaped my consciousness.

I cannot imagine, O God, how I could have set out on my journey of fatherhood, much less single fatherhood, without you as the force for both patience and celebration at the foundation. Your supportive presence has made me more understanding of my children, more amazed at the wonder of being human, more capable of having fun with them, more likely to be forgiving of myself when I have blundered parentally (and otherwise).

I am grateful for the increasing numbers of fathers who have given up the sexist notion that only mothers can rear children; who, as single men, have chosen to adopt children; who, when fleeing an unhealthy marriage, do not flee their children as well. I admire these men who go against the societal grain to keep building their lives around their children. I am inspired by those men who either share fully with their ex-spouses the demands and joys of child-rearing or who take on the role of full-time single parent.

I have taken delight in my children through all the phases of their maturation, and the finest treasure in my storehouse is the continuing joy of being Dad to children who are now adults. Indeed, you have drawn me to a place of enrichment, O God. How can I but thank you?

Amen.

ONE
Anticipation

Dear Son,

You came into the world very much wanted and eagerly anticipated. I know I don't look very happy in the picture your mother took of me painting your nursery furniture, but that frown wasn't because I lacked enthusiasm about your imminent arrival; it was because your mother had just, moments before the picture was taken, insisted that I put one more coat (the tenth I think!) of that ultra-white enamel (nontoxic, of course) on the used furniture she chose over new stuff. She said the older furniture, as long as the crib bars were close enough together, had much more character than anything new she looked at, and HER baby was going to have character in her or his (we had no idea which until the doctor held you up by your heels) furniture.

So there I was painting the crib and the little chest and the changing table. Your mom might have insisted that, for the final coat, all brush strokes had to go in the same direction—even in those damn little nooks and crannies. She thought my looks of pouting and frustration were cute back then, so she snapped that picture. Anyway, the next time you run across that shot you'll understand my facial expression and why I'm holding my arm at that really odd angle.

I/we really were more than excited about your growth and development in your mother's womb and every little sign that your exit was coming sooner and sooner. Also, you should know that I became an overprotective and worrisome father long before your birth; that wasn't a new part of my personality that just happened upon me the first time you wanted to spend the night away from home.

We lived close to several hospitals when your mom was pregnant, but in the mix was the hospital with one of the finest neonatal intensive care units in the country. That's the one we chose as your place of birth. We didn't anticipate that there would be any problems with your delivery, but why not choose the best facility for emergencies in case one came up?

Your mom chose her obstetrician based on the fact that his reputation was strong and that he delivered at that hospital exclusively. We chose your pediatricians because one of their team was a leading neonatologist who cared for newborn babies with extra struggles at that very same hospital. Actually, choosing the pediatricians took more time than your mother took selecting her obstetrician; that's because we did interviews.

You were in utero when SIDS (sudden infant death syndrome) first became widely publicized nationally. It was an extremely frightening prospect for all parents of infants and parents-to-be. I wanted to find a pediatrician who would be diligent in looking for even the slightest sign that you, when you were ex utero, might have a breathing irregularity. In my trying to explain to the doctor at an interview what my concern was, he somehow got the idea that I thought I myself might eventually be the victim of SIDS. And he said to me, almost as if I were one of the little boys on an exam table, "No, Mr. Farmer, I think you are a little too old now to be taken by SIDS. You shouldn't worry one little bitty bit."

Your mother's face turned bright red from embarrassment, and then she and the doctor had a great laugh together before he assured me he'd be overly thorough in watching for anything odd in the Farmer baby's respiratory processes. Though embarrassed myself, I heard the true concern in his voice that I was looking for, and we chose he and his team for your care. They were great.

Once we got you here, we wanted you to be able to enjoy fullness of health, and though we were poor, poor graduate students, your mom and you had the best medical care available anywhere. Because we loved you before we ever saw you and wanted the best for you before we even knew whether you'd need a boy's or a girl's name, we were arranging for the best we could possibly provide for you long before we ever laid eyes of amazement and delight on you.

Love, Dad

• • •

The LORD appeared to Abraham by the oaks of Mamre, as he sat at the entrance of his tent in the heat of the day. He looked up and saw three men standing near him. When he saw them, he ran from the tent entrance to meet them, and bowed down to the ground. . . . Then one said, 'I will surely return to you in due season, and your wife Sarah shall have a son.'—Genesis 18:1–2, 10

• • •

Gracious God,

This was joyous anticipation. It was not a segment of time lacking in ample anxieties, but, nonetheless, was filled with utter joy. For nine months, in an ongoing series of thoughts and celebrations and investigations well-known to you, I wondered about who this person would be and about every single aspect of our imminent acquaintance—including whether the baby would be female or male.

You were present with me when I first began wondering about his health and hoping that while his mother carried him, even then, he would do well and come into the world without any kind of health condition that would in any way diminish his ability to enjoy his life. You heard me in my prayers asking for strength and insight to point him to you and your love so that there might never be a moment in his life at which he would have to wonder about your loving embrace of him.

You saw the lists I made about attributes and habits of mine that needed to be adjusted or alleviated if I were to be the best example I could be for him. I won a few and lost a few, but not for lack of trying.

With all my thinking and planning and imagining, I was still unprepared for the thrill that overtook my reasonable anxieties (to some degree!) when I felt him moving inside his mother. Thank you, Gracious God, for traveling with me on my initial journey toward fatherhood.

Amen.

• • •

From a Shilluk creation myth:

> And so it came to pass that Juok, creator of life on earth, wandered here and there throughout the world. And as Juok wandered, he said to himself, "The earth is now a better place because I have fashioned human beings, both men and women, out of the different soils I have created. For they alone are able to speak and to shout, to sing and to dance in both joy and sorrow. And they alone are able to make the earth grow green and gold with food for those who live on it. The men and women whom I have fashioned are perfect human beings, and my heart is happy with all that I have created.
>
> *Source:* "The Creation of Human Beings," in Donna Rosenberg, ed., *Folklore, Myths, and Legends: A World Perspective* (Lincolnwood, Ill.: NTC Publishing Group, 1997), 6.

TWO
The Mystery of Life's Beginning

Dear Dr. Holt,

I don't know what your theological convictions about birth are or even if you frame what you do day in and day out in a theological framework. You already know my bias, so it won't surprise you to hear me saying, "I saw God at work in that moment." At the very least, you remain amazed at the wonder of birth; I sensed that in the superb care you gave my wife during her pregnancy and in your mannerisms and attitudes in the delivery room. I am so very grateful for all you have done for us.

I will never forget the moment of my son's birth and the fact that you had a key role in bringing him into the world. I saw human life begin as a slippery, screaming flash of flesh in your hands and, then, suddenly in mine.

That birth changed my life in every imaginable way. Nothing about me will ever be the same again.

These few days into my son's life I'm still dumbfounded by the wonder of it all (and, well, mildly sleep deprived). He absolutely amazes me.

I sincerely hope our paths cross again. Whether or not that happens, you will always be the recipient of our family's collective gratitude.

Gratefully,
David Albert Farmer

• • •

In those days a decree went out from Emperor Augustus that all the world should be registered. This was the first registration and was taken while Quirinius was governor of Syria. All went to their own towns to be registered. Joseph also went from the town of Nazareth in Galilee to Judea, to the city of David called Bethlehem, because he was descended from the house and family of David. He went to be registered with Mary, to whom he was engaged and who was expecting a child. While they were there, the time came for her to deliver her child. And she gave birth to her firstborn son and wrapped him in bands of cloth, and laid him in a manger, because there was no place for them in the inn.—Luke 2:1–7

• • •

Gracious God,

How utterly remarkable that I have seen life come to be and now hold in my arms its miraculous confirmation. The full meaning and joy of holding my baby surely escape me; I am overwhelmed.

He is so intricate, so fragile, so satiny, so inextricably connected to my heart, just as five tiny fingers grip one of mine. I will not, cannot, forget this encounter and the touch of perfect softness in my hands; this attachment is forever. And the kiss to the tiniest of foreheads causes me to realize how devoted I will be in enhancing every aspect of this child's, my child's, well-being, development, and happiness.

Thank you, God, for the singular thrill of this unrepeatable moment. Thank you, God, for this view of life.

Amen.

• • •

The British Prime Minister Tony Blair and his wife Cherie are celebrating the birth of their baby son who will be called Leo. He is the first child to be born to a serving British Prime Minister for more than 150 years and was named after Mr. Blair's father. The latest addition to the Blair household arrived at 0025BST and weighed in at 6 lbs. 12 oz., according to Downing Street. An emotional Mr. Blair said he was thrilled at becoming a father again and praised the doctors and midwives who assisted his wife.

Source: "2000:Blair's Delight at Birth of Fourth Child," *BBC On This Day*, May 20, 2000, http://news.bbc.co.uk/onthisday/hi/dates/stories/may/20/newsid_2510000/2510429.stm.

THREE
Nonstop Reasons to Rejoice

Dear Son,

The divorce happened about half your life ago, but its shadow has impacted you as if your home were always broken. You have slipped so quickly into young adulthood that I forget to remind you of important facts you need to carry with you for the rest of your journey.

Your mother and I weren't always at odds with each other. The little bit of time we had before you arrived and most of the time up until several months before we separated were filled mostly with joy for all of us.

Look back at the pictures from your early childhood. Look at the smiles, including yours. Those were real smiles, smiles that formed on our faces (and not just in front of the cameras) because we all loved each other and had loads of fun and took delight in being a "traditional" family.

Look through your "baby book" and the amazing scrapbooks your mother kept of all your "firsts." Look at her joy in those pictures; look at mine. And notice our pride too!

Somewhere there's a picture of me in scrubs, holding you when you were minutes old, right after the nurse bundled you up. That was the SECOND time I held you. No one was there to take a picture when the doctor who delivered you handed you to me. I was the first person ever really to hold you in any kind of nurturing way. The doctor held you before I did, but mostly by your ankles, and they wouldn't let your mom use her hands at that moment.

We were both present for all your "firsts," except one. We both got weak-kneed when we were invited to observe your circumcision. Jewish parents seem to have no trouble with it, but we were thoroughly Gentile about the whole thing. I apologize for abandoning you at that moment. I was just across the hall, if that helps, and I ran to your side when I heard you cry. (I don't know why I thought you wouldn't cry. The doctor had said something about this new device he used that caused "almost no pain.") Anyway, I hope you agree by now that our decision to have that done has made your life a little easier.

There was your first injection, your first pair of "big boy" shoes, your first haircut, your first party, and on and on. Every one of your firsts was the most significant first that had ever taken place anywhere, anytime. Your mom captured it all on film, and then she created these heirloom scrapbooks to preserve them. Look at the pictures. Look at the smiles. YOU were our joy.

The divorce changed the way your mother and I felt about and related to each other, but not one tiny bit of delight in you ever escaped. Our broken home brought broken hearts, but no loss of love for you—not even for a day. Remember that every morning.

Love, Dad

• • •

Abraham gave the name Isaac to his son whom Sarah bore him. And Abraham circumcised his son Isaac when he was eight days old, as God had commanded him. . . . The child grew, and was weaned; and Abraham made a great feast on the day that Isaac was weaned.
—Genesis 21:3–4, 8

• • •

Gracious God,

Whether or not the process can be neatly designated as a "divorce," seeing parents pull apart from each other and give their children reason to believe that love for them will ebb away when it isn't being offered by "a team," children are, at best, bruised. I cannot hide behind my rationalizations when I commune with you. Some truths are bitter and cold, and facing them stings more painfully than unrelenting, blowing ice-snow in a winter windstorm.

Before my eyes is this child, trying to be brave and strong for the rest of us, but crushed by the announcement his mother and I thought we had planned so well. How could he have thought he caused OUR problems? My heart is breaking for him.

O God, if there is any way to ease his pain that is not occurring to me, I certainly look and listen for guidance. I know you will offer it if there is something more to be done. Thank you for your presence with him in his time of intense emotional pain.

God of love, how can I help him realize that he didn't cause his parents' problems, and, more pressingly, how can I show him that he is loved profoundly and that he is still the treasure he has always been to me? I want to show him that he, as well as his milestones, are still, and will always be, matters of HIGH CELEBRATION in our home. At present, neither words nor actions seem to be making the difference.

Our children remember our smiles, our embraces, and gifts we give them; and they see the same in the photos we keep for the scrapbooks, but they do not realize, it seems to me, the magnitude of how we love them and how we celebrate all about them until they become adults and, maybe, until they have children of their own (if they ever do). Even if I had words to express the depth of all I feel about him, I suspect that he couldn't absorb it all. Maybe, somehow, he will be able to feel more than he can hear. Maybe, somehow, I can show him, at all the right levels, what my limitations keep me from being able to say.

Amen.

• • •

Every day is truly a gift with our children.

Source: Al Freedman , "Giving Thanks," *Daily Life*, http://www.fsma.org/freedman04.shtml.

FOUR
Damned Divorce

Dear Mom and Dad,

It wasn't that I suspected you'd be angry with me or critical of me; you've always been completely supportive of me, regardless of what turns my life took. The thing was, I think, I didn't know how to tell you; my awkwardness and uncertainty were related to that. I knew the marriage had problems in it, as I thought almost all marriages did, but I was unaware that our problems really couldn't be fixed for a list of reasons as long as the years we were married.

In any case, I'm more grateful than I will ever be able to say that the very first words out of your mouths were words of complete understanding and support. Thank you for not being critical of anyone; thank you for not trying to explain the situation in your own words; and thank you for leaving God and sin out of the discussion. God is still right in the middle of the whole thing, and no sin has been committed by anyone.

I'll tell you all else I know when I get home for a face-to-face visit. I need to be in my family circle now, and I want the kids to feel firsthand the reality of family love all around them as well. We'd like to head down there within the next two weeks, as soon as school and work schedules can be juggled.

Love, David

• • •

Words attributed to Jesus in the Fourth Gospel:

Everything that [God] gives me will come to me, and anyone who comes to me I will never drive away.—John 6:37

• • •

Gracious God,

Anybody but me, God. Anybody but me.

I hated the single life: I never wanted to go back to it. Not even a bachelor's party the night before my wedding. What was there to celebrate?

Me, the family man. Now no spouse with whom to share my life. Now a broken home for my children. Now a new identity for which I had never prepared myself.

People are looking at me differently, Lord. They really are. And I am looking at myself differently too.

I feel so guilty. I feel like such a failure. But you know as well as we knew that this relationship died. Is there any way I can let go of this guilt?

Someone at church told the children that if Mommy and Daddy had only learned to pray together and never go to sleep angry, this wouldn't have happened. How ironic.

We did pray together, and we were rarely angry with each other. Our parting was amicable. There was still love, but it wasn't marriage-love anymore. The more serious problems couldn't be fixed; we tried so diligently. The last months were filled more with grief than anything else; we knew the marriage had died, but we couldn't walk away from it.

Right now, I don't know how, but I know with certainty that you are still walking with me. No doubt, that's how I've made it through the painful times on the way to this point in my life. I'm a divorced man, and you haven't given up on me, God. That more than anything else helps me move ahead.

I am so torn and heavyhearted right now. But I still feel gratitude to you.

Amen.

• • •

Your reaction to divorce is yours. While there are common stages, how you go through them depends on you. Having knowledge and tools can help you navigate your way through treacherous waters, but it will not magically take away the pain or fear.

The dangers you face in each stage are:

1. avoiding having to face or feel what you feel—you take the 'stiff-upper-lip' approach, numb out, live in your head, act as if nothing's wrong or that it's no big deal. You keep pushing painful feelings and thoughts aside.
2. getting stuck in the feelings, fears, betrayal, etc. and prolonging them.

Part of the challenge throughout this process is to experience the natural process of grief, rage, and letting go, while at the same time realizing that you do need to take back some of your power. Your feelings and thoughts are not the boss (even when they seem to be!). You are the person doing the work of grief and creating your life.

Source: Dawn J. Lipthrott, LCSW, "Stages of Divorce/Breakup," The Relationship Learning Center, http://www.relationshipjourney.com/divstage.html.

FIVE
"I Want Mommy"

"What do you mean, you want Mommy? Things are fine here; this is where you live most of the time. I'm here for you. Whatever you need I can do it for you."

"Nu-uh."

"What can't I do?"

"You can't be Mommy."

• • •

When her time to give birth was at hand, there were twins in her womb. The first came out red, all his body like a hairy mantle; so they named him Esau. Afterward his brother came out, with his hand gripping Esau's heel; so he was named Jacob. Isaac was sixty years old when she bore them. When the boys grew up, Esau was a skillful hunter, a man of the field, while Jacob was a quiet man, living in tents. Isaac loved Esau, because he was fond of game; but Rebekah loved Jacob.—Genesis 25:24–28

• • •

Gracious God,

I feel petty, God. I can't get past my child's honest feeling right now, my child's real need. My feelings are hurt. This is my time with my child. What can this child's mother do that I can't do?

Thank you, God, for your willingness to help me become adult enough to make easing this child's emotional distress my only real concern. I know what I need to say, what I should say; I need a push from you to be strong enough to say, "Well, if you want Mommy right now, we'll get you to Mommy as soon as we possibly can." And then, God, then I am going to have to swallow a big helping of inappropriate glee from my ex when I pick up the telephone receiver and call her to tell her what our child has said.

With your help, O God, I'm going to work at being thoughtful enough to want our child to be at as much ease as possible in being with Mommy or Daddy; we are not under the same roof anymore, but our child's love for both of us and need for both of us continue. After all, I realize that at my age I still want to be with my own mother sometimes.

With the strength you are offering me, I further seek to earn my child's respect and trust by helping and not hindering the ongoing development of his relationship with his mother. May I not in any way keep him from saying exactly when he needs or wants to be with his mother.

Amen.

• • •

I need some good questions or statements to give to a child that a year ago made the decision to live with his father and now wants to live with his mother. #1 reason: rules are too strict, etc. . . . in addition—mother might be moving to Arizona!" (we live in Michigan). PLEASE HELP!

Source: On-line posting at the Stepfamily Forum, January 20, 2003, http://ths.gardenweb.com/forums/load/step/msg0118071932394.html

SIX
Going to Hell
Jesus Is Very Uncomfortable by Now

Dear Mrs. Sharp,

I appreciated learning about my son's outburst in your Sunday school class the other day. When I first got your message, I was angry and embarrassed that he would act in such a manner at any church event, especially in your Sunday school class. I know that keeping seven or eight second-graders focused and well-behaved for a whole hour, week after week after week, is both tricky and demanding.

Believe you me, I immediately confronted him. The awkward part for me came when he told me why he wouldn't stop laughing no matter what you said to him and, in the process, got all the other children in an "unruly mood," as you described it. He told me you said to the class (and he says this is a direct quote from you), "All Jews are going to hell."

My son is exceedingly fond of his teacher at his elementary school, Mrs. Esther Cohen. He believes that Mrs. Cohen is one of the kindest people he has ever come across; my opinion of her ranks way up there too.

He also knows that my dearest friend in this city is Rabbi Edwards. We lunch together regularly, undertake projects to help unify—rather than further divide—people in our city, and have even been known to pray together occasionally. I have never had any sense that God disliked the Rabbi or that I'd miss him in the mass of humanity in God's more direct embrace in the next realm of life.

With all due respect for your opinions on this matter and with appreciation that you want the children to grow up confident of the importance of what Jesus has shown the world about the one true and living God, I strongly disagree with what you said about all Jews and hell. I'm especially concerned that you feel the need to lay such a heavy and negative burden on young, impressionable minds. I hope that you and I can sit down and talk about this issue. And on a related note, we need to talk about the appropriateness of talking about hell—divine punishment, rejection, eternally burning fires, etc.—with eight- and nine-year-olds. That kind of thing can even keep an adult awake at night!

In the meantime, may I ask a favor? Can you choose those stories for your Bible lessons that focus on God's love for all people? No hellish stories and no casting God in a mode of one who causes damnation?

Even if you and I are never able to arrive at a point of agreement on these subjects, I absolutely affirm your right to hold to your opinion. In the context of our congregation, my impression is that it would be a much better topic in the adult discussion forum. Children, for the most part, don't know that they can or should disagree with you.

My son's laughter was his way of disagreeing with something you said that seemed entirely unbelievable to him. He didn't understand how rude his laughter was to you, and he plans to apologize for that when he sees you again. But he, unprompted by me, thinks you are wrong and that your view is hurting many other people. Knowing Mrs. Cohen and Rabbi Edwards, as he does, and balancing that against some very mean people he has seen behind the scenes of church life—as only a PK (Pastor's Kid) can see—he was amused to think that really good people go to hell and really mean people go to heaven because of a "badge" they wear.

At first, he really did think you were trying to joke in some way. He asked me at lunch on the very day the incident took place, "Daddy, wasn't Jesus a Jew?" I told him that, indeed, Jesus was a Jew and proud of his Jewish heritage at that. He followed with another question, "So did God make Jesus go to hell?"

"Hell no," I said.

Thanks for taking the time to read of my concerns. I look forward to our face-to-face conversation.

Sincerely,
David Albert Farmer

• • •

What then are we to say was gained by Abraham, our ancestor according to the flesh? For if Abraham was justified by works, he has something to boast about, but not before God. For what does the scripture say? 'Abraham believed God, and it was reckoned to him as righteousness.' . . . 'Blessed are those whose iniquities are forgiven, and whose sins are covered; blessed is the one against whom the Lord will not reckon sin.' Is this blessedness, then, pronounced only on the circumcised, or also on the uncircumcised? We say, 'Faith was reckoned to Abraham as righteousness.' How then was it reckoned to him? Was it before or after he had been circumcised? It was not after, but before he was circumcised. He received the sign of circumcision as a seal of the righteousness that he had by faith while he was still uncircumcised.—Romans 4:1–3, 7–11a

• • •

Gracious God,

I long for the day when thinking persons at least can let go of religious superstition and the need to try to make you human and petty like some of us, with a need to punish those who don't see or understand life as we do. May I be a small force to promote unity among people and a theological foundation based on your love for us rather than your presumed hatred of us?

I'm so heavyhearted when I face the reality that Jesus lost his life for trying to get this point across, and while many more people have taken note of Jesus' teachings since he was executed, too few of us get them. We try to make Jewish and Christian scripture products of the modern Western world, and many of us have crippled ourselves with the ideas that whatever is inspired must be literal and that truth cannot reside in symbols.

We frighten our children and one another by feeling free to direct your anger, your "wrath" toward any people who see you in ways other than our ways. We have created communities of "faith" in which most people fear you and live their lives with the threat of eternal damnation hanging over them. Few people known to me have ever fully affirmed your love for them, much less your love for others.

We have drawn hell as a real place on our map of human geography, and in trying to deal with our own anxieties about the possibility of ending up in the lakes of fire for eternity, we try to divert our fears by sending everyone we don't like or understand to such a place of eternal horrors.

I am grateful that my son laughed at fearmongering and bad theology.

Amen.

• • •

While the Catholic Church regards the saving act of Christ as central to the process of human salvation for all, it also acknowledges that Jews already dwell in a saving covenant with God.

Source: "Reflections on Covenant and Mission," Consultation of the National Council of Synagogues and the Bishops Committee for Ecumenical and Interreligious Affairs, August 12, 2002, http://www.jcrelations.net/en/?id=966.

SEVEN
Ebony and Ivory

Dear Mr. Reidlinger,

Thanks for the strong academic and community-building leadership you provide for the students at Jean Gordon Elementary School. I love opening assembly every morning, and you may have noticed that I rarely ever just drop off the boys for school anymore. I get a lot out of watching the students, my kids especially of course, and your interaction with them. Those assemblies and my morning coffee really get me going. Besides the fun feel of the assemblies, it's great to know what's going on at school, and it's great to witness your affirmation of the children.

Since this is our neighborhood school, I never gave any consideration to what specifically was going on here before enrolling the boys to attend. As our house is only a few blocks away, I just knew the boys would attend Jean Gordon when they were old enough.

I had heard a few people make very positive, though very general, comments about the school. Now I have my own ideas about why things work so well here.

I feel so fortunate that my sons get to attend a school in which you have such strong racial balance on the faculty and in the student body. I have recently learned that, as a magnet school principal, you can "fill out" the student body with children from outside our area whose parents apply for openings for their kids. It's remarkable to see racial equality symbolized so positively and so powerfully when all the students and teachers are gathered outside for their morning assembly. And the highlight is when you have them sing along with Stevie Wonder and Paul McCartney, almost once a week I think, "Ebony and Ivory."

Thank you for creating the perfect way for my children to continue growing up color blind.

Gratefully,
David Farmer

∙ ∙ ∙

The following day they came to Caesarea. Cornelius was expecting them and had called together his relatives and close friends. On Peter's arrival Cornelius met him, and falling at his feet, worshiped him. But Peter made him get up, saying, "Stand up; I am only a mortal." And as he talked with him, he went in and found that many had assembled; and he said to them, "You yourselves know that it is unlawful for a Jew to associate with or to visit a Gentile; but God has shown me that I should not call anyone profane or unclean. So when I was sent for, I came without objection. Now may I ask why you sent for me?" Cornelius replied, "Four days ago at this very hour, at three o'clock, I was praying in my house when suddenly a man in dazzling clothes stood before me. He said, 'Cornelius, your prayer has been heard and your alms have been remembered before God. Send therefore to Joppa and ask for Simon, who is called Peter; he is staying in the home of Simon, a tanner, by the sea.' Therefore I sent for you immediately, and you have been kind enough to come. So now all of us are here in the presence of God to listen to all that the Lord has commanded you to say." Then Peter began to speak to them: "I truly understand that God shows no partiality, but in every nation anyone who fears [God] and does what is right is acceptable to [God]."—Acts 10:24–35

∙ ∙ ∙

Gracious God,

It seems as if very few people in your world are paying any attention to the reality of racism and all of its debilitating effects within the cultures of most, if not all, the nations of the world. Not only do bigotry, hatred, and violence grow when we keep our racism alive, but also, with racism, we build barriers between ourselves and you.

We need help, O God. Lots of help. Serious help.

Amen.

• • •

Founded in 1994, the Harmony Movement encourages Canadians of all racial, cultural, and religious origins to embrace and promote harmony, diversity, as well as equality. Members of the Harmony Movement hope to dispel myths about prejudice in our society. We want Canadians to experience and appreciate the many faces, the many voices, and the visions that make up the human landscape of Canada. The Harmony Movement believes that everyone must make an effort to eliminate the barriers to mutual understanding so that our differences can be recognized and respected.

The Harmony Movement is the recipient of the 1999 Award of Distinction from the Canadian Races Relations Foundation (CRRF) for its innovation and excellence in race relations practice, as well as for its creative use of art to combat racism.

In 1997 the Harmony Movement commissioned twenty-four leading Canadian photographers to create a national photographic exhibition that expressed some of the diverse realities of the people of the country. Literary works from twenty-four esteemed Canadian poets and writers complement the photographs.

Source: http://www.harmony.ca.

EIGHT
To Share or Not to Share

WHY IS IT THAT JOY AND EXCITEMENT can be doubled or tripled when you get to share it with someone who cares a lot and understands at least a little?

The dogs seem elated with the excellent and unexpected news of his promotion, and the kids are as excited as young teens get about anything unrelated to appearance or peers. But there is a void because there's no one to talk to who grasps the long years of sweat and lateral moves he took to get positioned for just this appointment. And who was close by to identify with his sighs of relief at how much easier it was going to be now to pay the bills and educate the kids?

He would go to bed that night—strengthened by the well-wishes of friends and long-distance family members, but there would be no one who had traveled alongside him for the long haul with whom he could share his pride and sense of accomplishment. Nor was there anyone to say, "Thanks for all your hard work for me, for us." A happy morning became a lonely evening.

• • •

For God alone my soul waits in silence.—Psalm 62:1a

But he said to me, 'My grace is sufficient for you, for power is made perfect in weakness.'—2 Corinthians 12:9a

• • •

Gracious God,

It's silent all right, but I want the silence to be a pathway into your presence, not another reminder of how lonely I feel. It is so difficult to feel like the Lone Ranger, especially at such key junctures. Thank you for your never-failing companionship.

Amen.

∙ ∙ ∙

The first night my son and I spent in our new home, I put him down in his spartan little crib in the barren little house in a run-down neighborhood, and he began to cry. So did I. I wept huge salty tears all into his soft baby hair, and told him it was all a mistake, a misunderstanding. Mommy didn't understand what she was losing; she was just confused and all. I'd call her tomorrow and we'd work it all out. We didn't. We couldn't, really. How do you work things out between two parties when one of the parties isn't the same party who made the agreement? In other words, she wasn't "her" anymore. For the most part, she was now, or on the way to becoming, someone entirely different, and this new person was no more the woman I married than a snake is its shed skin, or a butterfly is the caterpillar that it was.

So life began again for me. Parenting was not totally novel to me; I had had plenty of experience in raising my boy. For the most part, life continued the way it had since she got her evening job, about a year before we split up: I'd come home from work and take care of him until bedtime, then I'd go to bed. The difference was, I no longer had a partner to talk to, someone to plan and dream with, not even a few times per week. So my next big challenge was to determine what my new hopes, dreams and aspirations were.

Source: William VanSickle, "Is There Life after Divorce?" Responsible Single Fathers, http://www.singlefather.org/carticles/lifeafterdivorce080801.htm.

NINE
Visits Back Home

Dear Mom,

We got back home from our drive late last night. It was a good trip for us—lots of fun, laughter, requisite arguments between the kids, a vomit break for the dog, and some good talks, lots of good talks. For some reason, the three of us do some of our best heart-to-heart chatting on those long drives between here and there.

Anyway, after all these years, Christmas still just wouldn't be Christmas unless I got to spend at least a few days with you all. As you can tell, the kids feel the same way. Their enthusiasm for being with you and Dad, uncle and aunt and cousins never, ever wanes. They don't mind at all leaving their local friends behind for the wonderful fuller-family-togetherness with you all, the whole of our true family.

Thanks for the great gifts! How thoughtful (as always). You overdid it (as always). Thanks, too, for all the hard cooking work you did so that we could indulge ourselves in family treats and traditions—with extras for the trip and back here at home. Most of all, I thank you for the love you're able to show the kids, so they never feel like outsiders in the larger family that they, like I, get much too little time with. Your touch with them is just as magic as it was (is!) with your own children. I love how you love them.

The only problem any of us has is that leaving is awful every time. That never seems to get any easier or better.

We are truly gifted, and you are a great part of that giftedness.

Much love, D

• • •

She opens her mouth with wisdom,
    and the teaching of kindness is on her tongue.
She looks well to the ways of her household,
    and does not eat the bread of idleness.
Her children rise up and call her happy.—Proverbs 31:26–28a

∙ ∙ ∙

Gracious God,

You draw us toward joyous and meaningful experiences. I thank you for the many gifts of family—especially, today, for my mother.

I'm so grateful for the love felt and demonstrated in the home in which I grew up, and what riches to have the same family who loved me love my children also. The bond between Mom and the kids thrills me.

Her love for them, and Dad's too, extends the parental love and support undergirding them and enriching them. My life is enhanced as I feel the strength of love back and forth across generations.

Though the distance between us causes me to miss them tremendously, I am grateful that their interest in us never fades and that they are willing to be active in caring and communicating.

Amen.

∙ ∙ ∙

No matter how far grandparents and grandchildren live from one another there are two things working in their favor that can help to keep their bond alive and kicking.

First, young children have the ability to expand time. Remember when you were younger how time moved more slowly, and the streets seemed wider, the buildings bigger? This means the time you spend alone with your grandchild is savored by the child, and can nourish your grandchild for a considerable period. Second, believe it or not, technology is a blessing. It has become a great asset in helping to foster emotional relations over distance. Sure, technology can't help to soothe a fevered brow, go fishing with a grandchild or help out a harried parent, but it can be a boon to foster ongoing communication—the most indispensable factor in keeping grandparent and grandchild as close as possible no matter how far apart they live.

Source: "Long-Distance Grandparenting," The Foundation for Grandparenting, http://www.grandparenting.org/long-distance,htm.htm.

TEN
First Date . . . in a Loooooooong Time

OK, ENOUGH REALLY WAS ENOUGH. He had to get himself up out of there and take the date. The invitations had been coming rather steadily for a while, and he was the last person in the world who believed he should wait a little longer before thinking again about dressing up extra special, splashing on a little of the expensive cologne he loved, having a meal out at some place besides McDonalds, and enjoying a dinner companion in his own age bracket. It was now time to let himself remember how much he loved romance: date planning and hand-holding and kissing and, well, you know. It was time to head in that direction again.

• • •

> Very truly, I tell you, you will weep and mourn, but the world will rejoice; you will have pain, but your pain will turn into joy.
> —John 16:20

• • •

Gracious God,

The mourning has been adequately acknowledged and expressed for now. I won't ignore it or run from it when it visits again. Life is still a gift, however, and there are new and renewed celebrations to be relished. Thank you for the chance to learn to love joy again—maybe even with a special friend.

Amen.

• • •

Grown-ups have friends also. It is important that you tell your children that you have friends that are not only the same sex as you but also the opposite sex as you. If you have younger children, you may want to explain it to them in terms of friends, but if you have older children, you may want to explain it to them more as a need for a relationship. Older children will generally understand that you need something more.

It is not expected that the children will be thrilled about your wanting to date. Most children have the hopes that their parents will eventually get back together. They may look at dating as you trying to get back at mom or daddy. Eventually they will come to grips with the fact that you need to begin dating and they will most likely accept it.

Source: "Telling the Children You Are Dating," The Better Divorce Network, http://www.betterdivorce.com/info/chsingle.shtml.

ELEVEN
Bad Dreams

"Son, I wish you could tell me what these bad dreams are about that keep waking you up. I think it may be those television shows about characters hurting and killing each other."

"Daddy, I told you it's not that. The Teenage Mutant Ninja Turtles rule! And they don't make me afraid of anything."

"Then what is it? This is the third time in the last couple of weeks you've awakened really scared; that worries me, and I want to help if I can."

"I really don't know, Daddy. Honest. If I knew what it was, I'd tell you. Can I just sleep with you tonight?"

"Of course you can! I want you to be right here beside me if that makes you feel better. Grown-ups have bad dreams, too, sometimes. I certainly do. It's not unusual; I only wish you didn't have anything that really frightened you or bothered you in any way."

"Me too, Daddy."

• • •

In the second year of Nebuchadnezzar's reign, Nebuchadnezzar dreamed such dreams that his spirit was troubled and his sleep left him.—Daniel 2:1

• • •

Gracious God,

I hurt for my child who is frightened after a bad dream; few experiences are worse than being terrified in the night. There is no possibility for clarity of thought in the darkness.

I'm touched deeply that my presence gives comfort and assuages the fear, for a time at least. Monsters, falling forever, loved ones dying—we, in the daylight, finally rationalize our way away from most of what scares us, but fear is real. And there is much in this world to fear.

One day my child will face fear separated from me; for now, though, I'll gladly come in the night when I'm called. Thank you, God, for being my strength and comfort when my dreams make me afraid.

Amen.

• • •

As the Simpsons face the apocalypse, Marge asks Bart if he's wearing clean underwear. "Not anymore," he says after a very brief reflection.

Source: The Simpsons, Episode AABF14, "The Good Book Leads to Bad Dreams."

TWELVE
Only Her Hairdresser Knows for Sure

Dear Carlos,

I received a letter from Megan after church a couple of weeks ago. It was a piece of construction paper, colored beautifully and folded in a neat square. Occasionally I get little notes from some of the Sunday school children, especially when they have talked that morning about loving their church and loving their pastor. But this note was much more than that.

During the week, Megan's Sunday school teacher, Linda Mayes, called to tell me that Megan had also talked with her about what, for Megan, is a dilemma, the same matter Megan brought to my attention in her very artistic note. I think she's handling her concern in a way that is exceptionally mature for a third-grader.

This past Sunday, I asked Linda to come with Megan to my study right after Sunday school and before church. They did, and I talked with Megan about her note and got her permission to share it with you. Someday I will show you the note; indeed, it is lovely, and I'll always keep it.

The problem, Carlos, is a unique problem for a single dad trying to raise a young daughter on his own—as you do so beautifully. I'm sure you won't be upset when I tell you what the problem is, and I want to tell you in Megan's own words. My words would only make the matter murky.

Your brilliant little girl's own words, shared with you by her permission:

Dear Pastor David,
Since you and Mrs. Pastor got a devors and you are a single daddy, can you please help me please. I love my daddy so much but he cant fix my hair and I dont like to go to church or schol it looks bad. Can you tell him how Love, Megan D

So there you have it, Carlos. Your little girl is growing up and missing her mother's touch in all kinds of ways. She was petrified at the thought of hurting your feelings.

This is a practical and easy matter to solve, my fellow single dad. I have absolutely no experience in fixing a little girl's hair, but I have a couple of practical suggestions to offer.

1. Maybe it's time for a new style for her, one that requires minimal care.
2. I'm sure whoever cuts her hair would take the time to show you both how to comb and care for whatever style you choose.
3. Maybe a female opinion at the stylist's shop could be helpful. If there are no family members available, I'm relatively certain that Linda would make arrangements to join you. She and Megan are very close.

In such a fine-looking family and one in which everyone gives so much attention to looking great, you didn't think your daughter would forget about that stuff, did you?

You're a GREAT dad, Carlos. Keep up the great work! And give thanks that the dilemma can be solved, for the most part, with a twenty-dollar haircut.

With admiration from your pastor and fellow single dad,
David

• • •

Words that Matthew's Gospel says are from Jesus—not words about hair, but you get the idea:

> Is there anyone among you who, if your child asks for bread, will give a stone? Or if the child asks for a fish, will give a snake?
> —Matthew 7:9–10

• • •

Gracious God,

Thank you for helping us single fathers learn the lesson that acquiring new skills is a required and ongoing part of being a parent under any circumstances, and of being a single parent in particular. All the manuals we read will never get us to the nitty-gritty advice about many practical realities. Little girls need their hair combed until they learn to do it for themselves.

We are grateful, O God, when we can let go of the illusion that all parenting skills are innate.

Amen.

• • •

A Man and His Children

A man does what he has the skills to do.
He has the ability to make children.
He does it easily in a few seconds.
His accomplishment shows in his children.
They are the image.
He was also made after the image,
doing things with his physical strength
and producing his children with ease.

Source: "Gospel of Philip," in Willis Barnstone and Marvin Meyer, eds., *The Gnostic Bible* (Boston: Shambhala, 2003), 283.

THIRTEEN
Morticia's Fierce Fans

Dear Madam or Sir,

I'm keenly aware that there is little or nothing you can do about this kind of thing after the fact, but because you are manager of the Cinema Multiplex, I still wanted you to know about this incident. This past Saturday, I brought my young children (ages ten and eight) to your establishment to see one of the many family-oriented films that you routinely offer. Thanks for keeping the films coming that we can happily and confidently bring our kids to see.

We saw *The Addams Family*, and it was great. My kids and I enjoyed it thoroughly, but not as much or, at least, not in the same manner as several women who sat on the row directly behind us. They were all dressed in black leather, and obviously loved Ms. Angelica Houston's Morticia character.

Beyond the content of what the ladies were saying, their chatter through the whole movie was distracting at best. It was very hard trying to keep two hands over the four ears of my sons at the same time, when I didn't want them to hear a certain segment of dialogue in the movie (my own answer to censorship) and/or commentary from the women behind us. I mean, my sons wanted to hear the movie as I did. I would have asked the talkers to shut up, but I was afraid of a "scene." I also would have come in search of a manager, but I couldn't easily have stepped over everyone in our aisle in order to get out and then back in—so I/we just put up with it.

I'm a concerned parent who wants as much wholesomeness as possible to pervade the way my boys learn to look at the rugged, real world. What they heard from our fellow viewers was too much for kids eight and ten years of age. The whole incident could have been avoided if those who talk out loud at a theater, whatever it is they're talking about, are excused from that viewing.

Sincerely,
David Albert Farmer

• • •

Train children in the right way, and when old, they will not stray.
—Proverbs 22:6

• • •

Gracious God,

Surely there is some beauty in and reason for innocence in childhood—at least as much as we parents can provide for our children. Growing up happens too quickly as it is, and the dark and painful parts of life become a part of consciousness and reality much too soon, never to be gone again.

Thank you for your willingness to guide me in my understanding of what is best for my children as I try to help them ease into the adult world whole and hopeful.

Amen.

• • •

Denver Catholic Register: A lot of comedy today relies heavily on vulgarity and profanity; what do you think of that, especially since you have been so successful without resorting to that?

Bill Cosby: Twenty years from now, what will vulgarity be? That's going to be a very interesting answer. I have no idea. People are used to it and using it more and more and it doesn't seem to be much of a fight with the media. Even in print . . . the words come out in our daily newspapers, it's on our talk shows, things that you just randomly turn on, the radio. The children hear it and, certainly, the children are saying it a lot easier, (even in) some of the programs that used to be children-oriented, the words are coming.

Source: From an interview with Bill Cosby with the *Denver Catholic Register,* conducted by Roxanne King, September 6, 2000.

FOURTEEN
Tuna Pile

Dear Dad,

I was remembering the other evening what a hard time Sis and I used to give you on those nights when Mom worked late, and you prepared dinner. Do you remember? Our beef (no pun intended) was that when you cooked, the menu was always the same: hamburgers and Campbell's tomato soup, hamburgers and Campbell's tomato soup, hamburgers and Campbell's tomato soup. If she worked late two nights in a row, hamburgers and Campbell's tomato soup. (In fairness, there was one occasional variation when you were in a cornbread mood.)

Anyway, all this came back to me the other evening when I cooked dinner for the kids, and they revolted—or maybe "protested" is a better word. I saw this recipe in the Sunday paper called "Tuna Pie." We all enjoy tuna, and it looked like something quick to whip up, so I did. Well, something didn't go quite right; I still don't know what it was, but when it was done, the tuna mixture didn't look a thing like it had looked in the picture. It couldn't be sliced into slices of Tuna Pie; instead, it had to be, well, spooned out.

Everything was fully cooked, and with the ingredients, it had to taste good; but when I served it, the kids just sat there and stared at it. Then, they stared at each other. Then, one whispered something to the other. Then, they laughed uncontrollably, fell out of their chairs, and laughed for I don't know how long.

I thought they had a little inside joke going on, which I thought at first I wouldn't intrude upon. Eventually, I couldn't resist. If something were that funny, I wanted in on it; I wanted to laugh too. So I took the bait and asked, "What in the world is so funny?" That made them laugh all the more, to the point that they couldn't even get words out.

Finally, one of them could speak. He said, "Daddy, we can't eat that!"

"Why not?" I asked. "It's good," and it really did taste just fine.

"Daddy, it looks awful. It really looks bad. You called it 'Tuna Pie,' but it looks like a big ole tuna pile to us!" Uproarious laughter from the kids.

It really did look awful, Dad. I had to laugh too. They talked me into a fast-food run.

McDonald's sold a few more burgers as a result of my culinary disaster. The dog was pretty happy too.

I should have done burgers and condensed soup. Thanks for all the cooking you did. At least everything always tasted good and looked like it was supposed to be eaten.

Love, D

• • •

My appetite refuses to touch them; they are like food that is loathsome to me.—Job 6:7

• • •

Gracious God,

We are most fortunate to live when and where we do and have so many food options and so much food availability. There are so many great things to eat, as long as someone in the house knows how to cook them!

We are mindful of the many, many people in the world today who have no eating options at all. There are no choices for them to make about food type, preparation, or presentation. Greed and cruelty, we have learned, retard or preclude the distribution of food that is available to feed the world.

Again, we are grateful that we can be so well nourished in our situation. And at the same time, we are grateful for the nourishment of laughter and the joy of sharing life together.

Amen.

• • •

Source: From an article for kids by Jacob Ludin, *St. Petersburg Times,* October 7, 2002. The article title alone is great!

"You wanna eat? You gotta cook!"
An excerpt:

You run home from school with your stomach grumbling from hunger. You walk into the house and smell the most disappointing aroma imaginable. Instead of pizza, your mom is cooking liver and onions!

Some children and teenagers take matters into their own hands: They decide what is for dinner and cook it themselves. These young cooks are never disappointed when they come home from school. They eat what they want and have fun preparing it.

FIFTEEN
I Need a Break

He went to bed that night more than exhausted. As a single dad, he was used to the physical fatigue at the end of a day; lack of physical energy wasn't unusual at all. But that night was different. ALL his energy sources gave off warning signals that they had run dry.

He had no emotional energy remaining. Sometimes he laughed to regain his energy. Almost every day one of the kids—or both—said something really funny. When all else seemed too stressful and overly demanding, discouragement setting in, the kids' quips and questions, sometimes intended to be funny and sometimes not intended to be funny at all, made him laugh. In that laughter, almost always there was a new burst of energy for him to be able to get back up the next day and try to be the best parent he could possibly be to the most incredible people in the world, who called him, "Daddy." Even that didn't work that night, though. He was in an overextended place, way out of bounds.

The spiritual strength on which he relied so heavily had been depleted too. There was no inclination to pray, not because he didn't like or trust God at the moment, but because even prayer requires a certain investment of energy. He had none.

He never remembered being at such a place in his life, and if he'd had the ability to feel anything at all, he would have been afraid. Mentally, his clear thinking sort of came and went. He wondered for a minute what in the world he would do if one of the kids had a crisis in the night. He might just as easily run out and lift up the front end of his car as gather the energies to change a wet bed, clean up the pizza that was only partially digested before checking out of one small tummy, or stay awake and focused enough to help one of the kids calm down after a bad dream.

This dad was in a danger zone, and he knew it. He realized in his exhaustion that for the sake of the children, he could never let this happen to himself again. As hard as it was to arrange for times and ways to be away from the kids for a little bit, he had to do it for everyone's sake. All he could do at that moment was to wish for one of his small family's occasional peaceful nights.

• • •

> In the morning, while it was still very dark, he [Jesus] got up and went out to a deserted place, and there he prayed.—Mark 1:35

• • •

Gracious God,

OK. I'm not exaggerating.

I've had it, Lord. You know (of course you would know) that I'm honestly near the end of my rope. (I thought I'd reached the end, but evidently there is still a small part for me to clutch.)

I need a break from being parental!

There is no more patience, none; no more energy—physical or emotional. I'm nonfunctional as a father right now, but . . . but I'm all my kids have. Still, if I don't replenish myself, my effectiveness can only deteriorate further; that would be a scary sight for all of us.

Gracious God, I need help in order to act on the insight you've given me. As tough as it is to arrange, I will work out some kind of reprieve from responsibility, however brief it may be.

Whoever made me think that I'm indefatigable, a real superman? I'm embarrassed that my pride allowed me to believe such nonsense and get to this point of near desperation.

Amen.

• • •

In a letter to her sister, Nettie, Celie recounts a conversation she had with her friend, Shug:

> You telling me God love you, and you ain't never done nothing for him? I mean, not go to church, sing in the choir, feed the preacher and all like that?
>
> But if God love me, Celie, I don't have to do all that. Unless I want to. There's a lot of other things I can do that I speck God likes.
>
> Like what? I ast.
>
> Oh, she say, I can lay back and just admire stuff. Be happy. Have a good time.

Source: Alice Walker, *The Color Purple* (New York: Pocket Books/Simon & Schuster Inc., 1982), 200.

SIXTEEN
My Child Is Caught in the Middle
▲

THE HOLIDAYS WERE APPROACHING, and amid all the joy of anticipating Christmas with children, there came the now requisite frustration of scheduling with his ex-wife. When the children were smaller, the debate had centered around where the children would awaken on Christmas morning—all excited and thrilled about their gifts. As the children got older, the arguments were related to who would get the kids long enough to make a holiday trip to be at one of the ex-spouses' family gatherings. The differences of opinion on the subject caused him a range of emotional responses from pseudo-cooperation to mild frustration to, "She makes me so mad I could spit!!!"

Although the once-married couple agreed every year not to get their children in the middle of these differences, they invariably did. And especially as the children got old enough to voice their own preferences, the politics of which parent would win became intense. Each parent would try to lure the children to the schedule/trip she or he preferred, and payoffs to the kids included more and better gifts at one of the two family gatherings, as well as the opportunity not to hurt one grandmother's feelings.

Christmas, therefore, always seemed to have at least a small dark cloud hanging over it, and sometimes an actual storm. The issue was never resolved. Even as adults, their children were still "demonstrating loyalty" according to which Christmas gathering they chose to attend, and the time came when it wasn't unusual for the children to decide to attend different ones.

• • •

Be angry but do not sin; do not let the sun go down on your anger.
—Ephesians 4:26

• • •

Gracious God,

I really thought we could do all this in a neat and tidy way. We were so levelheaded at first: divorce can't be helped; we will move through it; we will affirm and encourage our child every step of the way; we will fairly divide what we own; neither of us will blame the other for what has happened; our children will never be asked to choose sides; and all will be well.

Something's not working, though. Our children feel caught in the middle. Our children feel the need to say one of us was wrong, and the other right. Our children don't know how to be loyal to two parents who are no longer one flesh. We were always so careful to be unified in our parenting; to relate to one of us was, in most every instance, to relate to both of us. And even our time with "Mommy only" or "Daddy only" was never an experience of seeking to press them to like one of us more than the other.

Here we are. We are going our separate ways. We are still united in loving our children, but as to the direction of our respective futures and how we do everything—the little things and the momentous tasks—these differ. Our children do not know which way is right. They are caught in the middle.

Gracious God, may I find enough of your grace and an adequate measure of common sense not to allow our children to have to choose between parents? This can never be accomplished apart from your calming, healing presence. Thank you for your willingness to be here among us and for your extraordinary care for our little ones, who have this new and unfair burden to bear.

Amen.

• • •

Caught in the Middle provides support, education, and advocacy for children ages 4–18.

How do separation and divorce affect children?

A child experiencing the separation and divorce of parents often feels confused, scared, responsible, angry, grieving, and struggling between loyalty to both parents. This program will provide your children with the emotional support and the necessary skills to communicate and cope more effectively with the losses and challenges of their changing family. Your child will learn valuable skills to avoid being caught in loyalty conflicts between parents.

How does *Caught in the Middle* help?

Your child will learn:
- Valuable skills to avoid being caught in loyalty issues between parents
- How to communicate feelings and needs in a more appropriate way
- Problem-solving around expressing anger

You will learn:
- How to avoid putting your child in the middle
- How to separate parenting issues from those concerning your ex-partner
- How to reassure your children and understand their experience by learning to communicate in a more open, constructive manner

By opening lines of communication parents can separate their past spousal relationship from that of their ongoing parental relationship.

Source: http://www.anndavis.org/children-caught-in-the-middle.htm.

SEVENTEEN
My New Love Interest

IN THE FAMILY THERAPY SESSION, it all came out—too painfully to hear and much too real to ignore. His preteen son hated, truly HATED, the father's love interest. The wonderful person who had captured his heart was, nonetheless, according to his son: selfish, immature, invasive, and dumb. His father, he insisted, was showing his own brand of selfishness and shortsightedness by even thinking of tinkering with their postdivorce, fragile family structure. His father's love interest would disrupt all their lives and most especially would divert fatherly attention, already usurped to some degree by professional demands, away from him and his siblings.

Even the family therapist was surprised by the sudden display of anger and full-scale criticism of how the boy's father made decisions in all phases of life. Rebuffing a sibling's attempt to express an alternate opinion, the preteen boy in great pain railed against his father: "Damn you! Damn you! You don't care about anyone but yourself. None of us would be in this mess if it weren't for you. I hate you!!!"

His father's heart was fully pierced, and life itself, not mere blood, poured forth from the wound.

• • •

Children, obey your parents in the LORD, for this is right. 'Honor your father and mother'—this is the first commandment with a promise: 'so that it may be well with you and you may live long on the earth.' And, fathers, do not provoke your children to anger, but bring them up in the discipline and instruction of the LORD.
—Ephesians 6:1–4

• • •

Gracious God,

This is really tricky. I'm talking complicated! So what else is new, huh? I'm in love. Well, that's new. I'm head over heels in love, and you know how real it is.

But I'm petrified. Somebody doesn't like somebody! Child hates prospective partner. It could get worse. Prospective partner gets tired of animosity from child? Prospective partner ends up disliking the day-to-day thing with the children?

No coercion. No mind games. No dressing things up (like my kids would tolerate that kind of thing anyway!).

We're looking at the prospects of living together. There's very little out there one can use to spit-shine the rough edges of reality; it's like my nubby, unshaven face first thing in the morning.

Can love conquer all here, Gracious God? My love, I mean. I love every person in this would-be blend. Can that be sufficient?

If everybody doesn't click well enough, I feel I'll be the loser somehow.

Amen.

• • •

Nurturing is an important part of parenting. A parent nurtures a child by providing encouragement and enriching experiences. Nurturing also means showing love, support, concern, and understanding to yourself as the parent. If you do not take care of yourself, then how can you take care of your child?

Source: Annette Firth and Kim Gressley, *Healthy Parenting: Taking Care of Yourself* (Tucson: The University of Arizona College of Agriculture, July 1998), 1.

EIGHTEEN

A Very, Very Special Invitation to Come to School

Dear Dr. Farmer,

As you know from my two recent telephone calls, your son is continuing to have problems related to his inability to readjust after he and Nina broke off their dating relationship. Despite the fact that the breakup was mutually agreed to, or so I have been told by both parties, neither child is able to get back to "normal" school life. This has been made infinitely more difficult because they have almost all of the same classes together.

Although they are only freshpersons, their feelings were and are very real, and while I am sympathetic to both of them, their disruption to almost every class in which they are both enrolled has gotten to be entirely out of hand. Just today, Nina stabbed your son in the leg with a pencil after he had done something to aggravate her. The time has come when you must get more directly involved in the process of helping us correct this problem.

First, your son must be disciplined for his part in this episode. Second, the school nurse says you should take your son to his doctor to have the wound checked out. Third, I would like to have you meet me in my office in the presence of your son to analyze the situation. Please sign below to indicate that you have received this communication from me. I will contact you at your office right away to schedule this appointment.

Since this is a school for the arts, we have a somewhat unusual, though effective for our students, way of dealing with behavior problems. I will ask you to give some thought to this before our meeting.

What I will initiate when you come is a role play. We will ask your son to observe. You and I will role-play the pencil-stabbing situation. I will play Nina, and you will play your son.

Sincerely yours,
Helena Holladay

• • •

Be at peace among yourselves. And we urge you, beloved, to admonish the idlers, encourage the fainthearted, help the weak, be patient with all of them. See that none of you repays evil for evil, but always seek to do good to one another and to all.—1 Thessalonians 5:13b–15

• • •

Gracious God,

I just can't seem to get away from the notion that the person who stabbed my son in his leg is the party at fault. What am I missing here, God? I don't want him to grow up thinking he doesn't have to face responsibility for his unsuitable choices, but it seems to me that teaching him just to tolerate a kind of violence or physical abuse, as mild as the act is being viewed by everyone but him and me, will be to give him a terribly wrong message about his worth as a person. The doctor keeps talking about the potential seriousness of such a wound, and the school people keep vilifying my son for being the "stab-ee."

Now, he may have provoked her verbally in some way or hurt her feelings by wanting to break off their intense attachment to each other; I wouldn't rule out that possibility by any means. I'm very mindful of Jesus' admonition to "turn the other cheek" when accosted, and I'm not in any way thinking of advising him to seek revenge. I do, however, think he must learn that he deserves to be respected even when others around him are suggesting otherwise.

What kind of father would I be if I didn't speak up in his behalf?

I open myself as completely as I can, O God, for your word and your guidance.

Amen.

• • •

School communities need to make a clear statement that all people in their schools have the right to feel safe from physical and emotional attack. This means that behavior that is threatening, harassing, bullying, or dangerous will not be tolerated. It means that people who feel threatened, upset, or endangered by someone's behavior have both the right and the responsibility to speak up. It means that mechanisms that are clearly understood by everyone need to be in place to deal with problems that come up in a fair, open, and effective fashion.

At the beginning of each school year, a letter should go home to parents telling them to talk with their children about the school's Violence and Harassment Prevention Policy. Even younger children can be told, 'We expect you to be safe at school. If anything ever happens that makes you feel unsafe or unhappy, we want you to go to a teacher for help right away and to tell us as soon as you can. We also expect you to act in ways that are safe and respectful to other people. If you or the school tells us that you have threatened or been disrespectful to someone, we will work together to help you figure out how to solve problems with people in other ways.'

Source: http://www.kidpower.org/Articles/school-policies.html.

NINETEEN
Money, Money, Mo . . . ney

Hey Guys,

Summers are for sleeping late, I know, so I trust you'll find this note when you come in here to get some breakfast. Please call me at work when you've read it.

I'm still frustrated by the big arguments last night about money—who has what and what we can have and what we can't have. I have lots of sore spots when it comes to money matters, and instead of being up front about them—as I still have the tendency to see you guys as little boys who can't understand real-life stuff (sorry!)—I come across as close-minded and authoritarian. (I HATED it when my Dad used to bring one of our disagreements to a close by saying, "Because I said so," and I heard that slip out of my own mouth last night. Scary! That's really why I'm writing this note that we can talk about at dinner. OK?)

So here's the thing. We are a three-person, middle-income family living on a single income. It's tough. Sometimes, behind the scenes, I'm juggling like you wouldn't believe. (Thank goodness for "Quicken"!) Much of the time we are overspending and making up the difference with a credit card. That's very bad business, and it will catch up with us sooner or later—probably sooner rather than later. It's hard for me to say, "No," to either of you.

I work hard to make sure you have all you need and what you want. When one of you says something that sounds as if you don't appreciate what I'm trying to do and my high-pressure struggle to make things happen financially, I lose it. I'm really sorry for the yelling last night, and—from now on—I'm done with that nonsense (at least when it comes to money matters).

You know the story of my parents' financial tragedy when I was in middle school that resulted in the loss of our beautiful house, Mom's and Dad's dream house in a dream location. (It wasn't ever to be featured on *Homes of the Rich and Famous*, but it was fancy for us and something that

Dad, especially, was so very proud of. Losing it nearly wiped him out emotionally as well.) Anyway, for a couple of years, until they got back on their feet financially, we lived in a dumpy kind of place that I hated, and there was very little money for clothes and such. It is no exaggeration that my brother and I each had two shirts and two pairs of pants for school, and a suit for Sundays. (Every male over five years of age wore a suit to church on Sundays, no exceptions at our church.) And Sis, similarly, had two skirts, two blouses, and a Sunday dress. These were all the clothes we had; these were the only things hanging in our closets.

Needless to say, I never wanted either of you to experience anything remotely similar to that kind of situation. I never wanted you to miss having all you needed plus the extras, and I have worked very hard to try to make that happen. You all have so much more than most people in the world, and I somehow want you to realize that.

Bottom line: there isn't an endless supply of money coming in, and it's time each of us, me most of all, stopped pretending otherwise. From now on, I'm going to be very frank with you about money matters—not to worry you, but to make you aware of where our money goes and how much, if any, we have to spare. I suspect that you'll end up learning much more than you care to, and I also suspect that friction about money will come close to disappearing altogether.

Have a great day. I love you both very much.

Call me!

Dad

• • •

The LORD spoke to Moses and said, "I have heard the complaining of the Israelites; say to them, 'At twilight you shall eat meat, and in the morning you shall have your fill of bread; then you shall know that I am the LORD your God.'" In the evening quails came up and covered the camp; and in the morning there was a layer of dew around the camp. When the layer of dew lifted, there on the surface of the wilderness was a fine flaky substance, as fine as frost on the ground. When the Israelites saw it, they said to one another, "What is it?" For they did not know what it was. Moses said to them, "It is the bread that the LORD has given you to eat. This is what the LORD has commanded: 'Gather as much of it as each of you needs, an omer to a person according to the number of persons, all providing for those in their own tents.'" The Israelites did so, some gathering more, some less. But when they measured it with an omer, those who gathered much had nothing over, and those who gathered little had no shortage; they gathered as much as each of them needed. And Moses said to them, "Let no one leave any of it over until morning." But they did not listen to Moses; some left part of it until morning, and it bred worms and became foul. And Moses was angry with them. Morning by morning they gathered it, as much as each needed; but when the sun grew hot, it melted.—Exodus 16:11–21

• • •

Gracious God,

We struggle financially and, at the same time, have so much more materially than most people in the world can even dream about. I wish I and the boys could think more realistically about how much we do have, rather than how little we have.

We have enough. More than. We have more than enough, and, staying focused on you, we eventually will see that.

We will not intentionally set up idols to greed and materialism where we live, and we will do our best to be happy with "enough" each and every day.

Amen.

• • •

'My desire is but for a little thing,' said the young Fisherman, 'yet hath the Priest been wroth with me, and driven me forth. It is but for a little thing, and the merchants have mocked at me, and denied me. Therefore am I come to thee, though men call thee evil, and whatever be thy price I shall pay it.'

'What wouldst thou?' asked the Witch, coming near to him.

'I would send my soul away from me,' answered the young Fisherman.

The Witch grew pale, and shuddered, and hid her face in her blue mantle. 'Pretty boy, pretty boy,' she muttered, 'that is a terrible thing to do.'

He tossed his brown curls and laughed. 'My soul is nought to me,' he answered. 'I cannot see it. I may not touch it. I do not know it.'

'What wilt thou give me if I tell thee?' asked the Witch, looking down at him with her beautiful eyes.

'Five pieces of gold,' he said, 'and my nets, and the wattled house where I live, and the painted boat in which I sail. Only tell me how to get rid of my soul, and I will give thee all that I possess.'

Source: Oscar Wilde, "The Fisherman and His Soul," in Ian Small, ed., *Oscar Wilde: Complete Short Fiction* (London: Penguin Books, 2003), 121.

Unless one is wealthy there is no use in being a charming fellow. Romance is the privilege of the rich, not the profession of the unemployed. The poor should be practical and prosaic. It is better to have permanent income than to be fascinating. These are the great truths of modern life which Hughie Erskine never realised.

Source: Oscar Wilde, "The Model Millionaire," in Ian Small, ed., *Oscar Wilde: Complete Short Fiction* (London: Penguin Books, 2003), 235.

TWENTY

Who Opened the Window?

Dear Mrs. Buford,

Yes, I know that my son shouldn't have been climbing into your dining room window at 2:30 in the morning—or at any other time, for that matter. No, this isn't something, as far as I know, that he does on a regular basis; I'm relatively certain that this was a fluke in many ways. And no, I don't agree with you that if his mother lived with him, things like this would never have happened. I've yet to figure out how you knew anything about our family dynamics in the first place; that is another story and another series of comments.

As I told you on the telephone, I had no idea he was anywhere but upstairs in his bed, and no one—believe me when I tell you, NO ONE—could have been more shocked than I when the police officer pounded on my front door, jolting me out of a deep sleep, and telling me what my son had done as he pushed him into the house. I was certain it was a dream. I couldn't figure out for the life of me how he could be standing out in the cold when I knew very well that he was upstairs in his bed.

I'm very grateful that you and your husband agreed not to press the point beyond expressing your well-founded anger and frustration, even though the law rules out your option to press charges, because your daughter called my son and his sidekick, asked them to come over, and opened the window for them when they arrived.

Obviously, I can't speak for him, and of course, I don't know what was planned had they actually made it upstairs to her bedroom. I am certainly grateful that the officer confirmed the absence of alcohol and drugs and that none of our children were involved in those particular dangers.

Insofar as I can be in control of these matters, I will assure you that this will never happen again, though I won't be able to follow through with your suggestion that I chain him to his bed at night. I hope that your daughter will not call and issue future inducements. My son will be in touch with you in the near future to restate his apologies.

Regretfully yours, David Albert Farmer

• • •

Read "rod" in the following verse in a nonliteral manner:

> Folly is bound up in the heart of a boy, but the rod of discipline drives it far away.—Proverbs 22:15

• • •

Gracious God,

Surely, I'm not objective on this subject, but up until now, this son's behavior has been superb, A+ behavior. I can't be just imagining this.

I think now is the time I have to step up to the plate and take his side in an absolute and dramatic way—for him and all interested parties to see with absolute clarity. If he needs to be disciplined, I want to do everything in my power to enforce the discipline with grace. God, thank you for your willingness to help me see truth and reality if I'm not thinking clearly.

Thank you also for your gentle and loving way of showing me when and how I've made a wrong decision. May that model, rather than angry people, guide me.

Amen.

• • •

This excerpt from a letter placed on the Internet, for all who can read English to see, really scares me. From all indications, it's entirely authentic.

> I have also observed that these children who are disciplined God's way are sweeter and kinder to others, because they are less self centered. They are really different in personality to those children who do not receive this kind of discipline. I have heard it said of children, whose parents have changed their strategy to the Lord's way of discipline, that their children are totally different children from what they used to be. Praise the Lord! God's way is always best! The scriptures will not fail you!
>
> For more spankings for Christ's sake! Mary.
>
> *Source:* http://www.understandingyourbible.com/gracew36.htm.

TWENTY-ONE

They Skipped This in Parenting Classes!

Dear David,

Remember a few years ago when you brought Megan's hair dilemma to my attention? Well, thanks to you, we got that problem solved in relatively short order and without getting her a Sinead O'Connor or Grace Jones look. (No offense to either Ms. O'Connor or to Ms. Jones.)

We are now faced with a new inevitability, and before you get weak-kneed, as the father of sons-only might, let me just say that I have already solved my own problem. I'm only writing to pass along a tip in case you ever run into other families like mine—with a father rearing his daughter all by himself.

If you thought I was talking menstruation, you were absolutely right! Again, relax. I don't want your advice, but some other poor soul in your future may not know about the www.tampax.com Web site. I know you're laughing and wondering how strange my sense of humor really is, but I swear it's there. You should read it. You might learn something and/or be able to help one of your sons with his daughter's growing up processes.

I won't ask you to meet me for coffee to talk about this, but I'd love to know your reaction when you have the time to have a look at one of the most practical and real Web sites I've ever come across. Tampax.com and a weekend with her aunt downstate made Megan very calm about the whole process, and let me tell you, it's not nearly as embarrassing for a man to wait in line at the drugstore holding a box of "Tampax Silk" as it was when my mom used to make me walk to the drugstore to get them for my sister! And, not to overlook anyone, a female doctor for a girl without a mom is a GREAT thing.

I'm sure there's a sermon illustration in here somewhere. If so, feel free NOT to give credit.

Love from one single dad to another, Carlos

• • •

'Even though you had to go because you longed greatly for your father's house, why did you steal my gods?' Jacob answered Laban, 'Because I was afraid, for I thought that you would take your daughters from me by force. But anyone with whom you find your gods shall not live. In the presence of our kinsfolk, point out what I have that is yours, and take it.' Now Jacob did not know that Rachel had stolen the gods. So Laban went into Jacob's tent, and into Leah's tent, and into the tent of the two maids, but he did not find them. And he went out of Leah's tent, and entered Rachel's. Now Rachel had taken the household gods and put them in the camel's saddle, and sat on them. Laban felt all about in the tent, but did not find them. And she said to her father, 'Let not my lord be angry that I cannot rise before you, for the way of women is upon me.' So he searched, but did not find the household gods.—Genesis 31:30–35

• • •

Gracious God,

In a world where social and cultural separations between women and men have rightly been blurred and in some cases eradicated, modern persons have not been able to change biologically what is inherently and essentially "female" and "male." We are left to celebrate who we are physically; inconvenience doesn't shadow the miraculous. A woman's menstrual periods are signs of her potential ability to conceive and bear life.

Thanks to you, our careful Creator.

Amen.

• • •

Centuries ago, children often died very early, and so they were largely ignored until they had proven their ability to survive. Once they had, they quickly joined the ranks of adulthood. . . . They were married off as soon as possible, before untimely death might curtail a strategic alliance, and so that they could immediately get on with the duty of bearing as many children as possible in order to increase the odds of one surviving to carry on the bloodline. Young people of the middle and lower classes were even less durable than their wealthy cousins—a poor woman might bury as many children as she bore—and they went almost directly from swaddling clothes into the workforce, as young adults, at around the age of eleven or twelve.

Source: Catherine Orenstein, *Little Red Riding Hood Uncloaked: Sex, Morality, and the Evolution of a Fairy Tale* (New York: Basic Books/Perseus Books Group, 2002), 49.

TWENTY-TWO

Martha Stewart Sure Don't Live Here!
or
I Swear, the Underwear I Used as Pot Holders Were Clean!

▲

Dear Dr. Birch,

I have a therapeutic challenge for you. In our next family therapy session with you, I want you to solve our major family problem. If you can't solve it, then I guess we're going to have to go through the painful process of trying to solve it ourselves, but I'd much prefer to pay for rather than work for solutions. You'll let us know when we get there if you have any solutions for sale!

I didn't get any of the family neat genes. I realize that my Dad enforced chore completion while my siblings and I were growing up, but I always thought that someday, it would all click for me. Well, it still hasn't, and now that I'm full swing into this single parenting, it's really tough. We're all slobs. The boys say that when they stay with their Mom, everything "at HER house" is always neat and tidy. (That's still about a weekend a month!) At least half the time, our place is in some state of disarray; the dirty dishes are the worst.

Since I don't set the best of examples, I find it hypocritical to try to make the boys do what I don't do well, and—of course—I'm always trying to compensate for the fact that they live most of their lives with a dad and not a mom. But we have to find some kind of solution. I can't afford a maid service, and I don't think partnering with someone just because of domestic skills and leanings is a good enough reason to make a commitment. It's a real dilemma, and sometimes a day-by-day one.

The thing is, by the time we've all started the day at 5:45 and gotten through a full day of work and school plus after-school activities and night meetings, just getting dinner together and homework done are huge challenges. We're beat at the end of the day, and since none of us has ever bought into the "cleanliness next to godliness" thing, we deal with the clutter one more day.

Dusting gets done about once a month, vacuuming about as often. Clothes stay clean, but rarely make it from clothesbasket to drawers and closets. Dishes are done about twice a week, and the kitchen gets a good cleaning about once a week.

What would the health department say?

Drowning in disarray,
David Farmer

• • •

The LORD spoke to Moses and Aaron, saying: When you come into the land of Canaan, which I give you for a possession, and I put a leprous disease in a house in the land of your possession, the owner of the house shall come and tell the priest, saying, 'There seems to me to be some sort of disease in my house.' The priest shall command that they empty the house before the priest goes to examine the disease, or all that is in the house will become unclean; and afterward the priest shall go in to inspect the house. He shall examine the disease; if the disease is in the walls of the house with greenish or reddish spots, and if it appears to be deeper than the surface, the priest shall go outside to the door of the house and shut up the house seven days. The priest shall come again on the seventh day and make an inspection; if the disease has spread in the walls of the house, the priest shall command that the stones in which the disease appears be taken out and thrown into an unclean place outside the city. He shall have the inside of the house scraped thoroughly, and the plaster that is scraped off shall be dumped in an unclean place outside the city. They shall take other stones and put them in the place of those stones, and take other plaster and plaster the house.—Leviticus 14:33–42

• • •

Gracious God,

I chuckled when I read about the levitical leprosy house—certainly not because there's anything at all funny about disease, but because if a house could actually get leprosy, ours surely has at least a leprous flare-up rather frequently. So these days where do we find one of those priests who can heal a house?

God, no one appreciates a clean and orderly house more than I do, and few people have as few skills as I seem to, to be able to keep a house in that kind of shape. My boys appear to be taking after me in that regard, and I surely didn't want to pass along the messy genes. I'm pretty sure nothing much is going to change until I can change and be a leader in our home on that issue, not a hypocritical tyrant in dealing with the boys and their messy living spaces. Their futures will certainly be at least a little brighter if they can manage to keep house better than I can. I'm honestly concerned, and I seek your leading.

Amen.

• • •

- Find appropriate and dependable child care based on your children's ages and needs. Backup care eases stress in emergency situations.
- Plan family activities with your children. Camping trips, picnics, and outings to the zoo are budget-friendly and a lot of fun for everyone.
- Try to communicate one-on-one with each child on a daily basis. Ask questions and listen well.
- Enlist your children's help in making decisions. A chart designating everyone's chores and responsibilities helps clear up confusion and makes the household run more smoothly.
- Provide consistent and appropriate discipline that is fair and never physically abusive.
- When children ask about their other parent, talk to them calmly and openly in an age-appropriate manner.
- Strong and volatile emotions are normal after a separation or loss. Don't ignore your feelings. Talk to someone whom you trust.
- Pay attention to your physical health. Eat nutritiously, exercise regularly, and get enough rest.
- Manage your time to minimize your stress. Get the kids to help out with household chores. Cook and freeze meals in batches.
- Develop and maintain a social life for yourself. Reassure your children that your love for them has not changed but that you need to establish close relationships with other adults.
- Remember, to care for yourself is to care for others. Focus on the positive things you do—managing a household, working, developing a sense of responsibility and self-reliance in your children—and avoid feelings of guilt and inadequacy.

Source: http://www.familyserviceofbucks.com/upload/html/Familypage05.htm.

TWENTY-THREE

The "M" Word

Dear Chuck,

You're about as funny as a budget deficit! Why I told the Nominating Committee that you'd make a great youth leader, I've lost touch with.

I want to thank you from the bottom of my heart for feeling free to tell the young people that their pastor would be discussing masturbation with all the boys who attend the fall retreat. And my sons will be delighted to learn that you told the youth group I'd done such a good job teaching them that I'd be more than happy to help others as well.

Several possibilities occur to me:

1. I cancel my participation in the youth retreat at the last minute because of a pastoral emergency that I'm sure can or will happen if I need it to.
2. I attend the retreat, offer my opening words, and then turn the program over to you.
3. I attend the retreat, offer my opening words, and then show a video.
4. I attend the retreat, offer my opening words, and then explain that you meant to say "maturation," not "masturbation" when you gave a preview of my part on the program.
5. I just do it as you have promised.

I'll let you know what I've decided the morning before you all leave for the camp.

Just for the record, as progressive on all levels as I must seem to you, I'm kind of a shy guy who grew up in a home where sex wasn't discussed at all. The closest I ever came to talking to my Dad about sex was in the car one day. I must have been seven or eight years old. He was driving my aunt, who didn't drive, to the grocery store. I asked him, "What is 'circumcision'?" I'd heard the pastor mention that word in a sermon; he'd gone on and on and on about "circumcision" and "uncircumcision," and God seemed to be all for circumcision and all upset with uncircumcision.

Honestly, Dad nearly drove off the road. His face was bright red, and when he swerved back into the flow of traffic, he mumbled something about "talking to me about private stuff like that later." He never did, and believe me, for all my late father's exceptional qualities, I got the message not to ask again. (Imagine his response a few years later when I asked at a family dinner what the "F" word meant. I'd seen it written on a wall at school and had no idea even what part of speech it was—noun or verb. I did notice that it rhymed with "luck.")

My mother did check a book out of the Halls Crossroads Public Library for me once, and I appreciated the gesture. I read it, even though I was embarrassed that—as news traveled in a small town—everyone would know the one sex book in the library had been checked out by my concerned mother for me. The book, despite all the humiliation I was going to suffer at school and at church, really said no more than I'd already seen in the *World Book Encyclopedia*. (Did you ever see those clear page appendices? You know, with every page you turn, a different layer of a human body is removed. Clothes, then no clothes, then no skin, then no muscles, then no internal organs—only bones on the last page.)

OK, so I learned a thing or two by osmosis and vowed that if I ever had kids, they were going to get the facts about sex—mechanics and emotions—early on. And when we did have kids, I kept my word. The world had changed. The children's sections at Borders as well as Barnes and Noble blew me away. I bought my boys a sex book when they were about five and three.

It was a cartoon version of the facts of life, complete with anatomically correct drawings of all female and male body parts. Except for *Good Night Moon* by Margaret Wise Brown (which I read to one or both of them well over one thousand times), the sex book (the title of which I don't recall) was their undisputed favorite. They would laugh nonstop, for minutes at a time, every time I read the words "vagina" and "penis." It even became a little habit, after a while, that they would rush to say those words before I could utter them during the reading process.

To have been such a progressive dad to younger children, I think I abdicated later on. When sex came up in conversation, the boys seemed all too knowledgeable. Earthiness abounded. Sex education was a part of their elementary and middle school curricula. I'd signed papers giving them permission to participate in those classes. And there were television shows aired during early evenings with sexually based humor that both my boys seemed to "get." I don't recall ever having made sure they knew what they needed to know from an emotionally and physically healthy perspective.

What I did do, however, was to make sure that they knew of my more progressive attitudes about sexuality and sexual expression. The red flags I waved had to do with stories about people who were irresponsible sexually and who diminished themselves and used others in the process. We had straight friends and gay friends in our neighborhood and in our church. We had straight couple friends who were married and some who were committed without marriage. In the end, what I wanted for my boys, and I do think I made such comments on several occasions, was to keep themselves safe always and to see them set a goal of long-term (lifelong if possible, though that didn't work for me and their mom), monogamous and loving, sexual and emotional intimacy.

Having said all that, I'm back to where I began. Thanks for giving me this wonderful opportunity of talking to the male children of others about the morality of masturbation. I'll have great fun searching scripture for my text.

Please don't commit me to topics in the future; I'd really prefer to do that all by myself. Please expect to find the ball back in your court on a day and in a way that you won't expect.

Your pastor and onetime friend, D

• • •

What brainless wonder thought that this passage referred to masturbation anyway?

> Judah took a wife for Er his firstborn; her name was Tamar. But Er, Judah's firstborn, was wicked in the sight of the Lord, and the Lord put him to death. Then Judah said to Onan, 'Go in to your brother's wife and perform the duty of a brother-in-law to her; raise up offspring for your brother.' But since Onan knew that the offspring would not be his, he spilled his semen on the ground whenever he went in to his brother's wife, so that he would not give offspring to his brother.—Genesis 38:6–9

• • •

Gracious God,

So many people, including lots of monotheists, have really messed-up ideas about sexual expression, and we keep passing them on and around. We cause our children to think certain natural acts are disgusting and sinful. Verbally, or otherwise, we teach them that the best sex is almost always no sex, even as adults!

Outside religious circles, many people live as if no moral standards apply to any form of sex. Huge numbers of people are hurt, abused, and violated. So many of our human societies are utterly saturated sexually with all that is destructive and illicit.

As a result of these extremes, we have communities filled with sex offenders and sex addicts and persons in committed relationships who cheat on their partners and all sorts of people suffering with emotionally based sexual dysfunction.

If we could only go back to the beauty and simplicity of celebrating sex and sexuality in ways that demonstrate self-respect and respect for the one who is our partner in sexual intimacy. Can we?

Amen.

• • •

Where was I in that sixteenth year of my body's age, and how long was I exiled from the joys of your house? Then it was that the madness of lust, licensed by human shamelessness but forbidden by your laws, took me completely under its scepter, and I clutched it with both hands.

Source: John K. Ryan, trans., *The Confessions of St. Augustine* (Garden City, N.Y.: Image Books/Doubleday & Co., Inc., 1960), 66–67.

Boys [American Indians of the Kwakiutis nation] were honored with coming-of-age potlatches when their voices changed, an event which was referred to as "the boy's first monthly" (Ford 1941: 35). At this feast, the boy's father announced the potlatch position that his son would eventually inherit.

Source: Nancy Bonvillain, *Native Nations: Cultures and Histories of Native North America* (Upper Saddle River, N.J.: Prentice-Hall, Inc., 2001), 484.

TWENTY-FOUR
Ivory and Ebony

Dear Mr. Reidlinger,

We are doing our best to settle here in Baltimore. As you could have expected, we all miss New Orleans terribly, and the boys compare their present school very unfavorably to Jean Gordon. I'm not so sure that will change, but here we are.

A few years ago I wrote you a letter thanking you for the leadership you were giving to antiracism at Jean Gordon School and in New Orleans as a whole. I thought you might like to know how far your influence in that matter has now reached.

When we moved to Baltimore, I took my older son to his new suburban school to meet his teacher and his principal. The principal was a very kind man who took the time to show us through the school and to introduce us to key people. At the conclusion of this tour, the principal asked my son if he had any questions, and he said yes he did have one question (this out of the mouth of a fourth-grader influenced by you and the Jean Gordon community): "Why do Black people not like your school?"

"What do you mean?" the perplexed principal asked.

"Well, you showed us all the way through the school—every classroom, the gym, and the football field. There were almost no Black people anywhere around, so I was just wondering why they won't come to this school."

I was both proud and amused—proud of my son for missing the persons of color and amused at how flustered the principal was as he tried to explain that there simply were very few persons of color living in the area of the school and that if they lived there, of course they would be as welcome as any of the White students.

I believed the guy, but my son didn't. He just nodded to the principal as politely and as skeptically as a savvy car buyer who had just been told that the sale price on the vehicle is the dealer's cost.

While I'm writing, I have to tell you this related story that took place in a nonschool setting. Soon after our arrival in Baltimore from New

Orleans, an older church member invited the boys and me to lunch one day after church; she was most gracious in her offer, and we were happy to accept. We went to her "club." And we had a delightful meal together topped off by several of her life tales for dessert. We all left full and happy, at least that was my impression.

In the car on the way home, both boys sat in the back seat rather than going through the typical tirade about whose turn it was to sit in the front. I thought that was curious for sure, and equally as curious was the whispering conversation going on between them as we drove toward our place. Just about the time I was turning into our driveway, they said in unison, "Dad, we need to talk to you." (I knew immediately that whatever was on their minds had to be something rather serious, because "daddy" was for everyday and fun and love while "dad" was for business and trouble.)

"What is it, guys?" I asked.

"Can we have your permission never to eat at that place again?"

"What? Why? It was beautiful, and the food was great. You both cleaned your plates, a time or two!"

"Well, it wasn't the food."

"What was it, then?"

"Daddy, there were no Black people eating at that place, only White people."

"Boys, that's very sensitive of you to have noticed, but I'm sure I saw several persons of color there."

"Yeah, you did," one of them said. "And they were the people serving the White people their food."

Well, Mr. Reidlinger, I was pained at that moment that I, as racially sensitive as I take myself to be, had missed what they saw with absolute clarity; but I was also pleased that they did and told me so.

As I said in my letter to you on this subject while we still lived in New Orleans, I think you had a great deal to do with helping my boys grow up sans racial prejudice. I doubt that you have taken the time to think about how far and wide your antiracist words and ways have touched lives and changed people. Thanks again, from the heart.

Gratefully,
David Farmer

P.S. I told them, as you could have guessed, that they never had to eat at "the club" again.

∙ ∙ ∙

The God who made the world and everything in it, [the one] who is [Sovereign] of heaven and earth, does not live in shrines made by human hands, nor is [God] served by human hands, as though [God] needed anything, since [God] [Godself] gives to all mortals life and breath and all things. From one ancestor [God] made all nations to inhabit the whole earth.—Acts 17:24–26a

∙ ∙ ∙

Gracious God,

My children have taught me so much. I am grateful for their sensitivity to the reality of dignity for all people and for their keen eyes in searching out racism that tears away at inherent human dignity.

I am grateful for what they have shown me in this case and so very proud that they do not tacitly accept "the norm" as "the right."

Amen.

∙ ∙ ∙

The Anti-Defamation League (ADL) today expressed appreciation to those countries and leaders who strongly condemned the vehemently anti-Semitic speech by Malaysian Prime Minister Mahathir Mohammed before the summit of the Organization of Islamic Countries, but called those who acquiesced or were silent in their reaction to the speech, 'willingly complicit in spreading Mahathir's hate.'

Source: ADL Statement on World Reaction to Mahathir's Speech, October 17, 2003, http://www.adl.org/PresRele/ASInt_13/4375_13.htm.

TWENTY-FIVE
Sup, Docs?

Dear Dr. Schuberth,

As we pack up to make our move north of Baltimore, I wanted to say a word of profound appreciation to you and your colleagues for the excellent medical care you've given the boys for more than half their lives. Being a single dad, often with no one locally with whom I can discuss my concerns about their health, you've been an invaluable part of their healthy growing up years. My words are woefully inadequate to thank you for constantly going above and beyond the call of duty for them and for me, but I offer the words instead of driving away and acting as if all you did for us was just business as usual.

Now that my older son has reached a height of 6'5", towering over you and your staff and your patients, we often have a great laugh about the chat you had with us when he decided to become a vegan. You couldn't possibly remember this conversation, but you told him as a 14-year-old that one of the potential problems for teen vegans was stunted growth. Maybe the stunted growth possibility just skipped him, or maybe it was because he became Andrew Weil's most devoted teen follower. I think about that chat at least every time the three of us pack into the car for a road trip: me at 6'1", older son at 6'5", and younger son at 6'7".

I can also recall how hard it was for any of us to remember the younger son's knee ailment caused by Osgood Slaughters Syndrome. He once told the school nurse he had Oscar Mayer's Syndrome!

Seriously, you were never too busy for us. You always took the time to see the boys and to talk to them all along the way as real people. You always talked to me too, but never through me to them. They were clearly your patients and, in your approach, of primary importance. I thought it was a sign of your concern and competence when each boy got to the point that he felt confident about initiating a call to you or conversation with you directly.

For all your kindnesses, for all your care, for all your thinking ahead, for all of the sharing of your healing skills, I am grateful.

We will miss you!

With profound gratitude,
David Farmer

• • •

Epaphras, who is one of you, a servant of Christ Jesus, greets you. He is always wrestling in his prayers on your behalf, so that you may stand mature and fully assured in everything that God wills. For I testify for him that he has worked hard for you and for those in Laodicea and in Hierapolis. Luke, the beloved physician, and Demas greet you.—Colossians 4:12–14

• • •

Gracious God,

I am deeply grateful for those people who devote their lives to helping others find and enjoy fuller health. Thank you, O God, for your willingness to walk with us all, when we are well and when we are sick.

Amen.

• • •

One of the best ways to identify great doctors is to ask nurses in that field whom they would recommend. Nurses see both the professional and the human sides of doctors. They see firsthand how physicians handle medical crises, and how they interact with people. If I were moving to a town where I didn't know which pediatricians were great, I would call or drop by a labor and delivery unit, a newborn nursery, or a pediatric ward at a local hospital and ask several nurses for their opinions.

When considering a doctor, you want to think about four things:

1. Is he or she a well-trained physician who stays current with medical trends?
2. Does she or he practice medicine in a way that agrees with your philosophy of healthcare?
3. Does the Practice he or she is affiliated with fit your practical needs?

4. Will you feel comfortable asking this doctor any health-related questions that might arise?

Source: Alan Greene, MD FAAP, "Interviewing Prospective Doctors," June 13, 1999, http://www.drgreene.org/body.cfm?id=21&action=detail&ref=589.

TWENTY-SIX
The Best Sermon Ever

Dear Leila,

You're the greatest! I was thinking about you today and how much I appreciate you and have appreciated you across the years. As the boys have become young adults and are on their further spiritual pilgrimages now, they and I remember you as one of the most vital influences in their spiritual formation; you've probably been THE most significant influence on the development of their spiritual selves. I've thanked you from time to time across the years, and today I want to thank you again in a more detailed and formal way.

The boys brought with them, from New Orleans, a very rich foundation for healthy spirituality as a result of their years as a preacher's kid (well, that part didn't help at all in the long run) in the astounding faith community called St. Charles Avenue Baptist Church and, in particular, as a result of the special love, attention, and teaching offered to them by three gifted followers of Jesus: Ms. Brenda (Huffstutler), their children's minister; Ms. Ann (Madden), their children's choir leader and sometime Sunday school teacher; and "the other Ms. Ann" (Ernest), our minister of education.

The move to Baltimore was upsetting for our whole family. None of us wanted to leave New Orleans or St. Charles, but we all dutifully made our move. Except for the quick flight to Knoxville when Dad was suddenly dying, that drive out of New Orleans was the saddest trip I've ever taken.

The boys were crushed by the realities of divorce; we all were. But you were their Sunday school teacher and their friend through it all. You were there for them in ways none of the rest of us, including myself, could be.

You are walking, living, breathing affirmation, Leila, and with your help, the boys' lives and faith understandings grew and developed beyond their New Orleans years, despite the darkness of divorce. Every single Sunday morning they looked forward to getting to Sunday school to see you, that is, until the youth department drug them out of your children's division kicking and screaming (literally!) and forced them to meet with kids their own ages during Sunday school. (Nobody seemed to know that while the boys loved your Bible stories and your faith understandings, it was you they came to see. They weren't interested in so-called youth fellowship and having other kids' parents tell them about dating and life in general. They felt God's love in your presence, and that's what they wanted when they came to church. Imagine coming to church to be reminded of God's love. Novel idea, huh?)

To this day, they adore you. I know that almost every time they're in Baltimore to visit they still try to see you. I hope you know that those visits from them are not just celebrations of the friendship they have built with you post-Sunday school and post-Baltimore. When the foundations of their lives were crumbling, new boys in town with few friends and parents pulling apart, you embraced them with God's love, and every time they see you they know that it's not just you who loves them, but God. Your message to them has been more powerful and lasting for them than years of my sermons. Thank you, Leila.

There's something else I'd like to say while I'm writing, something else you did wonderfully for which I've never thanked you. When a divorce happens, and I've seen it happen countless times across the years with couples and individuals who have seen me for counseling, the people you've known as a couple are confused about how to relate to you and your ex independently of each other. What typically happens is they either "choose sides" or stop relating to either of you altogether. I was determined that this wouldn't happen to me, but it did.

I just wanted you to know that somehow you managed to love all of us—the boys, their mother, and me. You never took sides. You never caused the boys to believe that either their mom or I were in the wrong in any way. And you never built any barriers that made any of us doubt your friendship. I don't know anybody who can do what you did and still do. You have enriched my spiritual life too, and I'm grateful.

Love, David

• • •

People were bringing little children to him in order that he might touch them; and the disciples spoke sternly to them. But when Jesus saw this, he was indignant and said to them, 'Let the little children come to me; do not stop them; for it is to such as these that the kingdom of God belongs. Truly I tell you, whoever does not receive the kingdom of God as a little child will never enter it.' And he took them up in his arms, laid his hands on them, and blessed them.
—Mark 10:13–16

• • •

Gracious God,

I am so very grateful for people in the lives of my children who augment those essential values and attitudes toward life that I try to impart to them. I'm especially grateful for those who help bring to life the reality of your love for them and for all people. Utterly priceless gifts.

Amen.

• • •

Olsen Ebright, a 22-year-old college student, created a Web site listing the people who had been the greatest influences in his life so far. The following is a tribute to one of the top influences in his life, a Sunday school teacher.

I have had a lot of Sunday school teachers over my Methodist career. For whatever reasons, Mr. Rowe stands out from the rest.

I think the biggest advantage to going to one of Mr. Rowe's classes was they way he presented the material. The man was a lawyer, and from how good our Sunday school lessons were, a good lawyer.

The class would sit in a big circle around Mr. Rowe while he would walk around giving the lecture. In other Sunday school classes we would make a macaroni Jesus or something, but in this class we sat and listened.

Sitting and listening sounds boring, but imagine every Sunday, you got to hear the opening arguments for God. I felt like I was the jury in the Olsen v. God trial. Would I let God win me over in the case? The fate of my faith rested in the hands of God's lawyer, Mr. Rowe.

My favorite Mr. Rowe story is one that sticks out in my mind after all these years. The lecture was about being able to be yourself and not let others control you. I don't exactly remember the lecture, but I will never forget the end.

After the talk, Mr. Rowe walked over to the stereo and turned on *You Get What You Give* by the New Radicals. During the musical intro, Mr. Rowe walked back to the circle and stressed how important it is to be yourself. In unison with the opening vocals of the song, Mr. Rowe screamed, while counting off on his fingers, 'ONE, TWO, THREE, FOUR . . .'

I couldn't believe what happened next; Mr. Rowe, a charismatic 50-year-old man with faded gray hair, began dancing around the room singing to the song. As in 'dancing,' I mean the fullest possible meaning of the word. The class members didn't know what to do with themselves.

He started soliciting other people to join him dancing around the room. There were obviously no takers. He danced his way over to me and gave the look that said, 'Olsen, you better get your little butt off that beanbag and start dancing.'

In a moment of spontaneity, I sprang from the floor and joined in the madness. Soon the entire class was on the floor dancing. The entire second floor by now had heard the music. The volume was loud enough to reach the sanctuary on the other end of the first floor. The window into the classroom was filled with the eyes of curious adults wondering what in the world was going on in the high-school Sunday school.

Of all the Sunday school classes I have sat through, that is the only class I can still remember. I have to give Mr. Rowe credit for an amazing year at Linworth. To this day, I can't hear *You Get What You Give* without picturing God's lawyer dancing around a classroom full of stunned high schoolers.

Source: http://www.olsenebright.com/projects/top50/40_36/40_36.shtml.

TWENTY-SEVEN
A Death in the Family

Dear Son,

I'm sorry we couldn't get you out on a flight in time to see Dad before he died. A part of my shock still is how suddenly and unexpectedly it happened.

Your presence there meant a lot to me, and to the whole family. None of us will ever forget the extraordinary American Indian reading you did at the burial service. Thank you for the thought you put into that in the middle of juggling school while dealing with the shock of your grandfather's death and arranging for rapid transportation to be able to be there as soon as possible.

Dad loved you with great intensity, from the moment he first held you and every day since. The fact that you and he saw the world and theology from very different angles meant nothing to him in terms of his love for and acceptance of you.

He was actually very protective of you. He had no qualms about spanking me when I was growing up; I'm talking NO qualms. But I remember the first time he ever saw me slap your hand for continuing to do something I kept telling you not to do. You were in those wonderful two's, and you really didn't take directives from others very well at all. (No comment about whether or not that trait left you at three.) He jumped completely out of his chair and yelled, "You shouldn't be hitting that baby!"

I was in shock. I looked at him, finally, and said, "Dad, since when did you believe in 'sparing the rod'?"

"Since people learned better than to swat their young 'n's."

Point taken.

I know that you know he was your advocate, your patriarch, someone who found no fault in you. I also know that you know you will not have many people in your life who will love you with the intensity with which he loved you. I took great joy in the ways you always honored him, as you did when we gathered to say our earthly farewells.

I propose that we find ways to keep his love, his values, and his humor always alive somehow.

Don't grieve in isolation, and don't let the studies cause you to ignore your grief. We've had a huge loss here, and it hurts a lot; it should.

Love, Dad

•••

Dear Son,

As I look back on the last two weeks and review the saddest days in my life, what stands out, on the positive side, is that you walked through every step with me. You were a real source of strength to me as we stood around Dad's bedside that last time, saw the life-support equipment turned off, and waited with him as he died. I couldn't believe I was watching a real event. My heart was being ripped out as he eased out of this world and into the next one. Thank you, Son, for being there for me the way you always have.

Your dyslexia caused you so many frustrations and disappointments. Daddy never blamed you for any of your struggles, even if at points you stopped trying. He always said the problems weren't yours. "That boy doesn't have any problems in the world when it comes to brains. If he's not learning, they need to get him some teachers who can teach him in a way that makes sense to him." That comment was not only supportive of you; it was prophetic in ways. You know he was no educator, but he understood that you could learn whatever you wanted to learn provided the material was presented to you in ways that seemed relevant to you.

Man, oh man, would he get steamed when a teacher would criticize or punish you. He said he knew, even from several states away, that that teacher was an idiot. Some of them turned out to be, didn't they?

One of your greatest fans in the whole wide world is gone now. He had solid plans to be at your high school graduation in just about six months from now, and he was thrilled that you beat the odds and got yourself into college.

I can't believe he's gone. Our loss is a big-time loss, something I think we have to get used to but will never be able to get over. Your graduation day will be joyous, of course. We will hoop and holler and clap like nobody's business when you walk across that stage, but it will be a sad moment too. "That's my boy," he would have wanted to say.

His love for you won't ever die, Son. I hope you keep feeling it and especially that you feel it on the day of your graduation.

Thanks again for making your grandfather and your father so proud.

Love, Dad

• • •

Then he charged them, saying to them, 'I am about to be gathered to my people. Bury me with my ancestors—in the cave in the field of Ephron the Hittite, in the cave in the field at Machpelah, near Mamre, in the land of Canaan, in the field that Abraham bought from Ephron the Hittite as a burial site. There Abraham and his wife Sarah were buried; there Isaac and his wife Rebekah were buried; and there I buried Leah—the field and the cave that is in it were purchased from the Hittites.' When Jacob ended his charge to his sons, he drew up his feet into the bed, breathed his last, and was gathered to his people.—Genesis 49:29–33

• • •

Gracious God,

This grief business is debilitating. It has been my neighbor many times, but until now it never moved in to stay.

I'm trying to nurse my own grief while feeling the pain of my dear ones who also suffer grief. The pain is multiplied. These grandkids loved Dad like his own kids did.

He cared that I struggled as a single father. His interest and love and support made me a better dad.

I am so grateful for your presence with me and my loved ones during these days, and I am left speechless in the face of trying to express my deep gratitude that you were with Dad each moment of his life, including at the end of this earthly part of it. The only real relief I feel in the face of this grief is the confidence I have that he is more connected to you now than was possible in this realm of living.

Amen.

• • •

Signals for Attention from a Grieving Child

- marked change in school performance.
- poor grades despite trying very hard.
- a lot of worry or anxiety manifested by refusing to go to school, go to sleep, or take part in age-appropriate activities.
- not talking about the person or the death. Physically avoiding mention of the deceased.
- frequent angry outbursts or anger expressed in destructive ways.
- hyperactive activities, fidgeting, constant movement beyond regular playing.
- persistent anxiety or phobias.
- accident-proneness, possibly self-punishment or a call for attention.
- persistent nightmares or sleeping disorders.
- stealing, promiscuity, vandalism, illegal behavior.
- persistent disobedience or aggression (longer than six months) and violations of the rights of others.
- opposition to authority figures.
- frequent unexplainable temper tantrums.
- social withdrawal.
- alcohol or other drug abuse.
- inability to cope with problems and daily activities.
- many complaints of physical ailments.
- persistent depression accompanied by poor appetite, sleep difficulties, and thoughts of death.
- long-term absence of emotion.
- frequent panic attacks.
- persistent symptoms of the deceased.

Source: http://www.hospicenet.org/html/talking.html.

TWENTY-EIGHT
Reality Check

His teenage son hurried down the stairs and—somewhat breathlessly, certainly alarmed—he said, "Dad, Mom has cancer."

"What?!?"

"The biopsy they did, Dad, it was cancer. Mom has to have surgery right away, and then go for radiation and chemotherapy right after that."

"I'm so sorry, Son. I'm in shock."

"Dad, I'm scared. I don't know what to do."

"Well, you'll have to determine how to be there with her as much as you can, and then we'll have to figure out how to pray for her."

Ten years since the divorce, its own kind of radically surgical way out of a malignant marriage. Truth: no prayers for his now ex-wife in that decade, not a one he could recall. No way to clean up that failing.

Jesus' followers find ways to pray for even their enemies; his ex-wife was no happy recent memory, but she had been his spouse, and she was the mother of his children. Now her life was threatened.

Prayer as responsibility slapped him in the face. Followers of Jesus, without coercion, pray for all strugglers. No time for theoretical speculation about when and how to pray; it was now time for prayer, relational baggage notwithstanding, based on the best information and insight he had about intercessory invocation.

• • •

Words of Jesus as Luke remembered them:

> Love your enemies, do good to those who hate you, bless those who curse you, pray for those who abuse you.—Luke 6:27b–28

• • •

Gracious God,

I've been negligent, and I'm embarrassed that I stopped praying for the one who gave birth to these exquisite gifts from you, our children. I had wiped her out of my sphere of prayerful concern.

Now I must change my ways, not because I'm such a thoughtful or caring person, but because she's really ill. I must correct my omission, so this is the first prayer in a series.

I now add my positive energies for her wholeness to yours with confidence that you are working, and already have been working, toward what is good and whole and wholesome for all your children.

Amen.

• • •

No other factor is more important to the adjustment of your children to your divorce than the relationship you have with their mother/father. It is not divorce but a bitter and hostile relationship with your ex-partner that will damage your children. Get along with your ex and make doing so as important as maintaining a positive relationship with your children. You, your children, your ex, and society all win by your efforts to accomplish this goal.

Source: http://www.parentswithoutpartners.org/vaKnox.htm.

TWENTY-NINE
The Buggy

Dear Son,

I was pushing the buggy with your stash of this year's college survival stuff in it, helping you load your car before saying an end-of-summer goodbye, when I suddenly saw you—a full twenty years earlier—riding in the infant seat of a buggy just like the one I was presently pushing. Honest, I saw everything about you and our lives together over twenty years race through my mind's eye in a matter of seconds.

My mind saw, and my heart re-felt, the celebrations and sadnesses, the pullings together and the pullings apart that it took for each of us to get the other informed, equalized, and affirmed. The poignancy was astounding, but you didn't need a heavy dose of emotionalism from me before heading off to Europe for a year, so I smiled as best I could, told you how much I loved you (which was an understatement), and waved as you drove away to do your last-minute packing.

There's no way for me to tell you how time flies, and its speed is accelerating all the time. Those wise people who learn for themselves and advise others like me to cherish every moment are very wise people indeed. It's not that I have failed to cherish every moment with you; it's just that my cherish mechanism too often wanted to operate at full throttle only in retrospect. Also, I suspect that I sometimes muted my emotions a bit because how deeply I love you and your brother scares me.

The wait between event and full-feeling isn't as long as it used to be. I mean, with the buggy incident I was in touch with a host of feelings right on the spot.

I was overcome with the miracle of your birth as it was happening, but there was so much to take in about the wonder of you that it all didn't catch up with me until I put you in bed after your first birthday party. I walked right from your bed into the bathroom and cried my eyes out for an hour or more—scared your poor Mom to death. Those tears were a mix of joy and awe and pride and celebration and the fear of taking on the task of rearing the likes of you; they were feelings catching up with me.

Not only my arms but also my heart were wrapped around you from your arrival on. With the arms, I had to let go, but neither time nor distance will take you out of my heart.

On another continent, I hope you feel that love from your Dad. Keep taking good care of you, learn a lot, and the next time you notice someone pushing his son around in a grocery cart, remember that little boy once was you, and the doting dad was me.

Love always, Dad

• • •

> Listen, children, to a father's instruction,
>   and be attentive, that you may gain insight;
> for I give you good precepts:
>   do not forsake my teaching.
> When I was a son with my father,
>   tender, and my mother's favorite,
> he taught me, and said to me,
>   'Let your heart hold fast my words;
>   keep my commandments, and live.
> Get wisdom; get insight: do not forget, nor turn away
>   from the words of my mouth.
> Do not forsake her, and she will keep you;
>   love her, and she will guard you.
> The beginning of wisdom is this: Get wisdom,
>   and whatever else you get, get insight.
> Prize her highly, and she will exalt you;
>   she will honor you if you embrace her.
> She will place on your head a fair garland;
>   she will bestow on you a beautiful crown.'—Proverbs 4:1–9

• • •

Gracious God,

Just about the time I'm feeling confident as the parent of a firstborn, suddenly he's an adult, and the dynamics of the relationship change entirely. Oh well, new learning ahead.

I'm grateful that our connection is healthy and strong, having weathered not a few threatening adolescent gales. And I hope I've taught him well enough for him to face the world and its threats and demands and possibilities with resolve and confidence. You know, God, the most important lesson in my mind was the truth about your love for him and for all people; that to me is true wisdom.

I'm grateful for the beauty and wonder of his life today, continuing the blur of years and events that began at his birth. He is a baby and bright-eyed school boy and frustrated teenager and young scholar all at once to me; it's hard to take it all in, but I burst with joy at all that he is.

Amen.

• • •

I told my father not to worry, that love is what matters, and that in the end, when he is loosed from his body, he can look back and say without blinking that he did all right by me, his son, and that I loved him.

Source: Ethan Canin, 'The Year of Getting to Know Us," in Alberto Manguel, ed., *Fathers & Sons: An Anthology* (San Francisco: Chronicle Books, 1998), 27.

THIRTY
Moving Out

Dear Son,

I was crying the other day when you moved, with no ability whatsoever to explain why. No words would form in my voice box; it was paralyzed. I know that upset you, and I apologize for it.

It wasn't that the whole event was so sad. I mean, we'd have lots of adjusting to do after having lived together these years, often just the two of us. And I knew I was going to miss having you so close so often and taking almost moment by moment delight in all the things that interested and entertained you. But hell, you were just moving less than half an hour's drive from home to live on campus.

Your move was the most perfectly normal and natural thing in the world for you to do. So the sadness related to that adjustment, which seemed to come all too quickly, was only a tiny part of why I was crying. Mothers often shed the tears when a child moves out; fathers act stoic. For what it's worth, I did try not to tear up, as if to signal to you that what you were doing hurt me, that you'd made a choice that caused me pain.

I think you always have had more common sense than I have, and your perceptions of next logical steps in the growing up process came to you more readily than they came to me. I loved your childhood, but I was glad to let it go in exchange for the amazing friendship you offered me when you became an adult and put away childish things. That wasn't it, Son.

Most of my reason for crying that day was wonderment at what a choice young man you have become, right before my eyes, and the overwhelming gratitude I felt to have been granted the privilege of being your father. I might have lived multiple meaningful lives (were I a reincarnationalist) and never had the priceless gift of you as my son.

I'm glad you have a great new place. I hope my sunglasses covered my eyes sufficiently that you didn't have to explain an emotional father to your friends and roommates.

With all my heart, I love you. Dad

For everything there is a season, and a time for every matter under heaven: . . . a time to weep, and a time to laugh; . . . a time to keep silence, and a time to speak.—Ecclesiastes 3:1, 4, 7b

• • •

Gracious God,

My son is my treasure, and I can't imagine having lived without him. So often you have spoken to me through him. He has been a source of calm and common sense, of high points and hilarity.

Thank you for walking with him into adulthood and for the joy in him that I still cherish.

Amen.

• • •

Homer has Telemachus leave Ithaca, his home, on a journey to find the truth about his father's, Odysseus', fate. In the leaving and the returning, Telemachus the boy becomes a man. The sign of his adulthood was his beard.

'My dear child,' answered Eurynome, 'all that you have said is true. Go and tell your son about it, but first wash yourself and anoint your face. Do not go about with your cheeks all covered with tears. It is not right that you should grieve so incessantly; for Telemachus, whom you always prayed that you might live to see with a beard, is already grown up.'

Source: Samuel Butler, trans., *The Odyssey,* Book XVIII, by Homer (New York: Barnes and Noble Books, 1993), 228.

THIRTY-ONE
Closing Prayer ... for Now

THIS BOOK IS GETTING FINISHED in manuscript form right at the time my family and my late father's friends are marking the third anniversary of his death. Though he is no longer among us in physical form, there is no way I can write a book about anything that has to do with fatherhood unless I can, in some way, honor him.

That aside, I think it is an excellent exercise for all single fathers to think very carefully about their relationships with their own fathers and to pinpoint exactly what they have brought to the challenge of parenting from their dads. We humans are much more inclined to repeat what we've observed than to do what we read.

He was a GREAT dad, and he is missed with greater intensity than he would have imagined. I shaped my ideas about fatherhood by reflecting—sometimes consciously, sometimes not—on his strengths as a father to me and my siblings. I didn't like everything about his approach, but the overall effect was successful indeed; and I did like most of it, both while I was growing up at home and in looking back on my heritage as his firstborn child/son.

We were very different people and didn't have loads in common on the level of activities. He loved to fish and watch sports on television—especially the Atlanta Braves and the University of Tennessee football team. Other than that, he worked hard and went to church. That was about it, until . . . until he had grandchildren. Then it was as if his life started all over again.

Our relationship was strangely renewed as well. My older son was the first grandchild in the family. Finally, there were seven of them. Once grandchildren were in the picture, there was never a shortage of topics for conversation, reflection, and thinking ahead.

Once I left home for college, I never lived at home again, and, sadly, most of the years after I left, I lived at substantial distances from my family. Long before e-mail, we made good use of the telephone, though. Dad would never talk long on a phone call; in fact, nearly all his calls had simple, two-part agendas. The first part was always a general, "How is everybody?" He was really asking how everyone's health was; how school was for the kids; and how work was for me. He wanted rather pointed answers, usually. If he wanted more detail about anything he'd ask. Typically, the second part of these brief phone chats would be related to something he'd thought about, about which he wanted to say a word of encouragement or, rarely, offer a word of advice.

Conversations tended to run longer when the Braves or the University of Tennessee Volunteers weren't in season. In the off seasons, conversations might last upward to ten or fifteen minutes. He worried a lot about how I was holding up as a single dad and how the boys were holding up as children of a single parent. He wanted the boys to do well in school—as he had demanded of my sister, brother, and me.

He had grown up in abject poverty in a single-parent household; his mother had worked her fingers to the bone just to keep food on the table and a roof over their heads. She wasn't able to do that after a while, and his older siblings (he was the youngest of seven) had to drop out of school to go to work in order to keep the family afloat. He had been the only one afforded the opportunity of finishing high school.

Dad was my best buddy when it came to parent talk. He understood exactly how I felt about my kids, and he gave each of us regular words of encouragement. The business of being fathers had become our bond, and when we lost him at a very young seventy—suddenly and without any warning whatsoever—I lost my father AND confidant and the president of my sons' fan club. That void has never been filled, and it won't.

Nonetheless, I learned many things from Dad about the wonder of fatherhood. Most significantly, I learned from him the honor it is to be called "Dad" and the privilege it is to build one's life around providing for and loving the children with whom you are blessed.

To one of the world's GREAT dads and THE greatest to me, Thanks, Dad.

• • •

'Honor your father and mother'—this is the first commandment with a promise.— Ephesians 6:2

• • •

Gracious God,

My dad was a remarkable man, and I feel so incredibly fortunate to have known him, to have shared almost forty-seven years of my life with him, and to have been able to call him "Dad." Dad truly invested himself in the lives of his children and grandchildren. When he began counting his blessings, he didn't begin with finances or a new vehicle; he, without fail, began his list with Mom, his kids, and his grandkids.

Dad worked too hard trying to provide well for us, and I didn't understand that until I had the privilege of providing for my children. Dad never had a regret that he worked as hard as he did, however—only frustrations about how unsuitable "limited retirement" was.

He loved you, and he loved us; he reminded me to rely on your leading. What I observed in his fatherly ways meant more to me than any other source I consulted about childrearing. Such riches!

Amen.

• • •

We don't want to think about the death of our parents, even though we know the natural order of things is we will bury our parents some day. We push that thought way into the future. Although on one level we are prepared for their death, we really are unprepared for the actual death. It is beyond our comprehension that we will one day face the shock of their death and our knowing that we are now the grown up and may even be alone.

The intensity of our grief is dependent upon the circumstances of the parent's death, whether there are brothers and sisters, what your situation is in your life at the time the death occurs, as well as whether there is a surviving parent.

If the death of your parent is unexpected and sudden, your grief experience and period of adjustment will differ from those whose parent has been sick for a long time. Sudden death requires its own period to grieve due to the shock. Sometimes the sudden death is followed by feeling cheated out of enough time, and we become angry. We grieve for the special dates and events to come that we will have to face without our parent. Our expectation of the death of our parents is that it will only occur when they are very old, but even then our eyes do not perceive their aging. There is a deep feeling of regret that we were unable to tell them how much we love them and to tell them goodbye.

Source: Pamela L. Taylor, FDr., "Death of a Parent," http://www.goodgrief.net/deathofaparentpage.html.

Appendix

1. Don't order God around; get rid of imperatives in prayer.

There's a world of difference between, "Hey, Dad, get me a Coke," and, "Dad, could you get me a Coke when you run out to the store?" Think about it! The prayers that most people pray are nothing more, literally, than lists of orders for God. "Help me get a raise," "Make Aunt Ludie well," "Show me what to do," "Get me through this day," and so on. Doesn't that amaze you? What peers do we talk to like that, or even workers we hire to do repairs around the house? I don't regard order giving to be prayer.

I think the so-called "Lord's Prayer" as we have it in English leads many people to think in terms of prayer as giving God a list of things to do: "Give us this day our daily bread," "Lead us not into temptation"; you know how it goes. The theology of that prayer notwithstanding (God doesn't lead God's people into temptation!), those prayer forms are not in keeping with other prayers attributed to Jesus: "God, into your hands I commend my spirit," "Not my will, but yours be done."

2. Don't approach God as if God needs or wants to be appeased.

Keep in mind, despite what you may have been told (even all your life), that God is not small-minded, petty, grudge-prone, or moody. In order for God to be open and attentive to you when you come into God's presence in prayer, God isn't expecting any gifts and groveling from you.

Do you remember when God tried to communicate with Ezekiel, and Ezekiel went belly first onto the ground in a posture of fear and obsequiousness? Do you also remember what God said to him with Ezekiel's face in the dust? Underline this one in your Bible, Ezekiel, chapter 2, verse 1: God said (not with a human voice and vocabulary) to Ezekiel, "O mortal, stand up on your feet, and I will speak with you."

God doesn't expect to be appeased, though few people believe it. When you come to God in prayer, think Billy Graham, Cliff Barrows, crusade choirs, and the title—just the title—of the song they're singing at the end of every service: "Just As I Am."

3. Don't blame God for evil or tragedy.

If you are still reading the newspaper or the on-line news every morning (like you have time in the mornings!) with the assumption that everything about which you become informed has been willed by God in some kind of way, in any way, then your view of God is very negatively distorted. Even if you try to adjust your view of God a bit by thinking that God may have ALLOWED some evil event without CAUSING it directly, you still haven't left yourself with a very workable understanding of the one true and living God.

God has nothing to do with evil, period. God doesn't will it, cause it, or allow it. God doesn't work through evil, is simply not an accomplice to evil ever. If God wants to teach you something, it will never be through what is evil or tragic (even though God will certainly help us to move beyond our tragedies to life on the other side of despair).

God didn't "allow" the Holocaust. God didn't strike someone's child with a terminal illness in order to teach that parent some kind of lesson.

We simply can't assume that anything or everything that happens is God's will, intentional or unintentional; there are the realities of a physical universe (in which "errors" occur naturally) and of the power of individual and communal bad/selfish/evil choices.

God deals in goodness and truth, liberation and affirmation. That's it. The evil and the tragic are very real parts of our world and our personal lives as well, much too real.

God is leading us to combat and eradicate evil ("your will be done, on earth as in heaven"). Run, run, run from the Jerry Falwell approach to explaining 9/11!

4. Don't pray as if you have to talk God into doing what God hadn't already thought to do and isn't already in the process of trying to effect.

We don't have to beg God to try to effect healing when someone whom we love is ill. Prayer isn't a means to awaken God from God's divine dozing-off and tell God to get on with it. Before we ask, God's already at work to bring any and all kinds of healing and wholeness and goodness that are possible. Enter into prayer with that clearly in mind.

5. Don't bargain with God.

Okay, God isn't holding back on the healing or guidance or problem-resolution processes while waiting on you to make some big-time promises. God is working toward the good regardless of how much (or how little!) money you give to the church. God is Creator and Life-giver and Healer by nature; it is a logical impossibility to think that God can act in any way contradictory to who God is.

So you can promise never to miss Sunday school again or never to get drunk again, and—hey!—your promises, if you keep them, may make you a better person. But God doesn't enter into bargaining situations, largely because God's love for all God's children is unconditional. We can block the effects of God's love, but we can't negate the love itself.

6. Don't tell God what needs to be done in a given situation.

So many prayers that I hear (and prayers that I have uttered in years gone by) assume that God is either a dunce or a robot who cannot figure out independently (that is, without being told) what needs to be done to resolve a crisis. "God, this war needs to end, and here's what you need to do." "God, the hungry need to be fed, and here's how you can accomplish it." "God, I've got to lose some of this stress, and here's what you should do to make me stress free." Duh!

7. Don't treat prayer as incantation.

Prayer is not magic or magical. Prayer is nothing like and has nothing to do with casting spells. Learning and/or saying "just the right words" for the occasion is not a way to direct God's powers to your particular struggle. There are no required words, or more efficacious words than any others necessarily, for any particular type of prayer. God acts in love, not as a result of code words that would "tap" divine powers.

The apostle Paul recognized that many of our most meaningful prayers are wordless: "Likewise the Spirit helps us in our weakness; for we do not know how to pray as we ought, but that very Spirit intercedes with sighs too deep for words. And God, who searches the heart, knows what is the mind of the Spirit, because the Spirit intercedes for the saints according to the will of God" (Romans 8:26–27).

8. Don't think of God as your grandfather or your grandmother (or any other person or kind of person, despite *Oh, God* and *Joan of Arcadia*).

God is not a human being; God is Spirit. God doesn't "really" have eyes and hands and a voice and a throne.

God is neither female nor male; God is Spirit. God isn't limited by gender.

9. Don't treat prayer as a last resort, emergency measure.

Prayer is naturally a part of a healthy spirituality, including the spiritual reflections of seekers and skeptics. Communing with God is a way of life and isn't only attempted when someone is in dire straits.

10. Don't forget the fact that God is love—not just loving, but love.

If we keep this core, key reality in mind, then how we think about God, how we think about ourselves and others, and what we consider in prayer will change dramatically. "Now to [the one] who by the power at work within us is able to accomplish abundantly far more than all we can ask or imagine, to [God] be glory in the church and in Christ Jesus to all generations, forever and ever. Amen" (Ephesians 3:20–21).

• • •

1. Do base all prayer in praise of God.

This is the starting point of all authentic prayer. Whatever else we have in mind for our prayer session or experience, this is where we always begin. Paul's opening in his letter to the Ephesians is one of many examples from Christian scripture to help us begin and base our prayers in praise: "Blessed be the God and Father [Mother] of our Lord Jesus Christ, who has blessed us in Christ with every spiritual blessing in the heavenly places, just as [God] chose us in Christ before the foundation of the world to be holy and blameless before [God] in love" (Ephesians 1:3–4).

2. Do pray thankfully for what God has already done and is doing.

God is concerned about your situation or struggle, and God is already at work to pull you to wholeness/resolution when these are at all possible in the world as it is. Before taking the time to talk about how the ongoing struggle is impacting us—and that is something we should, indeed, do in prayer—we thank God for what God is already at work to accomplish. "God, we are thankful that as our sister faces this critical surgery you go with her and that her well-being is of utmost importance to you." "God, we are grateful that you have shown us the way of peace over and over again. How can we put into practice in this very real situation what we know to be right?"

3. Do pray as part of the one human family, recognizing that God neither recognizes nor approves of the barriers we human beings build between ourselves and other human beings.

Regardless of how hard it is for many of us to accept, God does not honor or recognize the barriers we build—racial, economic, relational, you name it. We are all members of the one and only human family. Enemies are real, but enemies are real people—at least in God's view—even if our hatred and/or fear of them cause us to make them soulless objects in our minds. God is more concerned with getting available food into the hands and stomachs of the starving third and fourth world people than God is with how well first world stock portfolios are doing.

4. Do pray directly to God, as Jesus did.

Jesus prayed directly to God, and so should we. We don't have to have a religious professional pray FOR us, and we don't ask our deceased loved ones to put in a good word for us with God. We may pray to God BECAUSE OF Jesus (that is, because of Jesus' take on God and Jesus' self-sacrifice in proclaiming God's absolute love), but we do not pray

THROUGH Jesus. Prayer is direct communion with God. Prayer is a twosome, not a threesome.

Of course others may pray FOR you—that is, may make you and your struggle a part of their prayer concerns, and you undoubtedly will make the concerns of others, especially your children, a central part of your prayers. But your prayers for your children are not their prayers, and your friends' prayers for you are not your prayers. Prayer is one-to-one.

5. Do pray with utter openness in God's presence, leaving "pretense" and "oughtness" on the game shelf. Express to God, with words if you can, what you think your hurts and needs are (without feeling compelled to force or obligate God to act in the way you tell God things need to be done, as suggested above).

Say what your real feelings are. Say what your real needs are. Be yourself. God loves you and loves you as you are.

You may not like how you feel about someone or some process. There may be times when you don't like yourself or something about how your child is living, but it's how you feel. God will hear, and God will lead you toward resolution of any and all things destructive.

6. Do pray as an active participant in what happens to you, your loved ones, and your world.

I can't see any real difference between "predestination" and "fatalism," except that fatalists don't seem to know who is doing what to them, and predestinarians blame God for everything. In both cases, the respective adherents take no responsibility for their own actions. They envision life from the perspective of a marionette. They are passive and powerless. They are lucky or unlucky, victors or victims through absolutely no involvement of their own.

You were created by God with the ability to think and act in your own best interest (and to your detriment if that's how you choose). Insofar as the political structures within the country in which you are a citizen permit your freedoms, there is nothing to stop you from being as proactive for the well-being of your child, of yourself, and of your fellow human beings as you choose to be.

Think of it this way. God isn't a finger-snapper, a forcer, or the enforcer. (The "enforcer" is the governor of California now, isn't he?) God invites, encourages, pulls, and embraces. You can accept and follow God's lead or not, but God has, without a doubt, empowered you to be who you choose to be.

7. Do pray with an awareness of God's extraordinary nearness.

God is not distant from you; God can't be. Given the fact that God expresses Godself, at least in part, as life itself, God is always as near to us as brainwaves and beating hearts and air to breathe and consciousness. If we do not sense the nearness of God's presence, there is a problem with how we feel or perceive, not with God's actual nearness. God is always at hand whether or not we're aware of it.

Permit me a modest anthropomorphism. I generally hate bumper stickers. I don't care if the lady in front of me has a kid on the honor roll of some school, whatever it is. I don't care (at least when I'm driving) if the guy who just passed me has his mother-in-law locked in the truck of his vehicle.

There are a couple of bumper stickers I've seen across the years that I do like, however. One of them says, "If God isn't close anymore, guess who moved."

8. Do learn from the prayers of others without being bound by them.

Prayers such as those in this book should be helpful, suggestive, instructive; they should be or become springboards. Prayer is YOUR conversation/communion with God. Treasure that and enjoy God's attentiveness to you; God is interested in all you need and want to say to the source of life and love.

9. Do listen for and watch for evidences of God's responsiveness to your prayers in new understandings that seem to come to you out of nowhere, in strong feelings you hadn't felt or noticed that you'd felt before, and in bursts of energy to act or to endure that you're pretty sure you couldn't have mustered all by yourself.

People who pray (TRY to pray, PRETEND to pray) by telling God what to do all the time are preoccupied with whether or not God is going to give them that Escalade or the Lotto jackpot. That, to them, is proof or not that God has answered their prayers. And when they don't get their way, it's really nice of them to make so many excuses for their god (small "g" intentional) who didn't fill their wish lists.

I don't think there is any such thing as an unanswered prayer. That would mean, in my understanding of prayer, that God was ignoring you; and that won't ever happen if prayer, for you, is openness to God, the honest seeking of God's leadership that I try to describe and demonstrate in this book.

10. Do set as your goal to pray without ceasing.

Praying without ceasing isn't talking to God twenty-four hours a day. It's a gradual adjustment of perspective about who God is, where God is, and how to commune with God in all of life. God is always with you, whatever you're doing, and as you affirm that, you sense God's presence wherever you go, eventually, easing into more focused communion with God as the most natural thing in the world.

- God is with us when we're celebrating the birthday of one of the kids at Chuck E. Cheese's or Billy Bob's.
- God is with us when we're counting coins to try to get through a very long month with some unexpected medical bills.
- God is with us when we must discipline our children and when we worry about war.
- God is with us when we're expressing ourselves sexually. (Oops! Viagra sales just skyrocketed!)

We don't have to get over to the church or pull off to the side of the road or kneel beside the bed to commune. Opening up to God in a focused, intentional, conscious way wherever you are—that is praying without ceasing.

www.ingramcontent.com/pod-product-compliance
Lightning Source LLC
Chambersburg PA
CBHW072010090426
42734CB00033B/2350